TIMED READINGS
in Literature
BOOK EIGHT

Edward Spargo, Editor

Selections & Questions
for this Edition:
Henry Billings
Melissa Billings

Fifty 400-Word Passages
with Questions for
Building Reading Speed

Jamestown Publishers
Providence, Rhode Island

Titles in This Series

Timed Readings, Third Edition
Timed Readings in Literature

Teaching Notes are available for this text and
will be sent to the instructor. Please write on
school stationery; tell us what grade
you teach and identify the text.

Timed Readings in Literature

Catalog No. 918

Copyright © 1989 by Jamestown Publishers, Inc.

Cover and text design by Deborah Hulsey Christie

Printed in the United States   HS

89 90 91 92 93 10 9 8 7 6 5 4 3 2 1

ISBN 0-89061-521-7

Contents

Introduction to the Student

These *Timed Readings in Literature* are designed to help you become a faster and better reader. As you progress through the book, you will find yourself growing in reading speed and comprehension. You will be challenged to increase your reading rate while maintaining a high level of comprehension.

Reading, like most things, improves with practice. If you practice improving your reading speed, you will improve. As you will see, the rewards of improved reading speed will be well worth your time and effort.

Why Read Faster?

The quick and simple answer is that faster readers are better readers. Does this statement surprise you? You might think that fast readers would miss something and their comprehension might suffer. This is not true, for two reasons:

1. Faster readers comprehend faster. When you read faster, the writer's message is coming to you faster and makes sense sooner. Ideas are interconnected. The writer's thoughts are all tied together, each one leading to the next. The more quickly you can see how ideas are related to each other, the more quickly you can comprehend the meaning of what you are reading.

2. Faster readers concentrate better. Concentration is essential for comprehension. If your mind is wandering you can't understand what you are reading. A lack of concentration causes you to re-read, sometimes over and over, in order to comprehend. Faster readers concentrate better because there's less time for distractions to interfere. Comprehension, in turn, contributes to concentration. If you are concentrating and comprehending, you will not become distracted.

Want to Read More?

Do you wish that you could read more? (or, at least, would you like to do your required reading in less time?) Faster reading will help.

The illustration on the next page shows the number of books someone might read over a period of ten years. Let's see what faster reading could

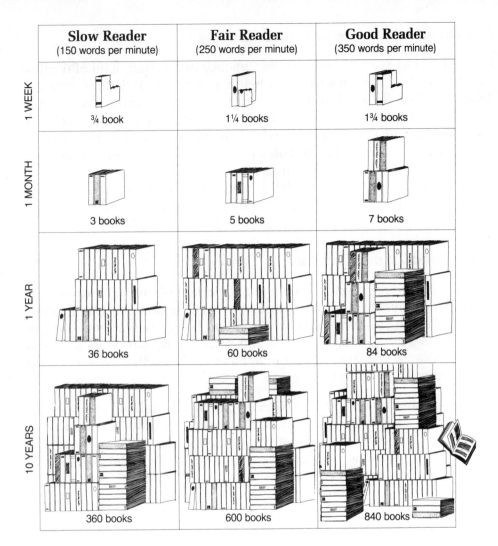

	Slow Reader (150 words per minute)	**Fair Reader** (250 words per minute)	**Good Reader** (350 words per minute)
1 WEEK	¾ book	1¼ books	1¾ books
1 MONTH	3 books	5 books	7 books
1 YEAR	36 books	60 books	84 books
10 YEARS	360 books	600 books	840 books

do for you. Look at the stack of books read by a slow reader and the stack read by a good reader. (We show a speed of 350 words a minute for our "good" reader, but many fast readers can more than double that speed.) Let's say, however, that you are now reading at a rate of 150 words a minute. The illustration shows you reading 36 books a year. By increasing your reading speed to 250 words a minute, you could increase the number of books to 60 a year.

We have arrived at these numbers by assuming that the readers in our illustration read for one hour a day, six days a week, and that an average book is about 72,000 words long. Many people do not read that much, but they might if they could learn to read better and faster.

Faster reading doesn't *take* time, it *saves* time!

Acquisitional *vs.* Recreational Reading

Timed Readings in Literature gives practice in a certain kind of reading: recreational reading. Recreational reading of novels and short stories is different from the kind of reading you must employ with textbooks. You read a textbook to *acquire* facts and information. That is acquisitional reading, reading that is careful and deliberate—you cannot afford to miss something you may be quizzed on later. Acquisitional reading speed must be slower than recreational reading speed.

The practice you will be doing in this book will help you develop a high reading speed suitable for literature.

Why Practice on Literature?

If acquisitional reading is so useful and important for students, why should you spend valuable class time learning to read literature faster? Shouldn't you be learning to read textbooks faster and better? Believe it or not, you are! That's right: the reading speed and skills you develop from this book will transfer to your textbooks and to other study reading. Here are some of the ways this happens.

1. The practice effect. In the dictionary, *practice* is defined as systematic exercise to gain proficiency. In other words, repeated drill brings improvement. You know from your own experience that when you practice anything—from piano to basketball—you become better at it. The same holds true for reading. As you are doing the drills and exercises in these books, you are practicing *all* of your reading skills at the same time. With practice you become a fluent reader and comprehender—a better reader of everything you read.

2. Using context. Good readers are aware of context and use it to aid understanding. Context refers to the words surrounding those you are reading. Meaning, you see, does not come from a single word, or even a single sentence—it is conveyed within the whole context of what you are reading.

The language of literature is rich with meaning. The storyteller is trying to *please* the reader, not *teach* the reader. The writer wants to share feelings and experiences with the reader, to reach him or her in a personal way. As you practice reading literature, you are developing your skill in using context to extract the full measure of meaning and appreciation. These same context skills can be put to work when you are reading textbooks to help you organize facts into a meaningful body of knowledge.

3. Vocabulary growth. Our early vocabulary comes from listening—to our families, friends, television, teachers, and classmates. We learn and understand new words as we hear them being used by others. In fact, the more times we encounter a word, the better we understand it. Finally, it becomes ours, part of our permanent vocabulary of words we know and use.

As time goes by, an increasing number of words is introduced to us through recreational reading. Most of the words we know come from reading—words we have never looked up in a dictionary, but whose meanings have become clear to us through seeing them again and again until they are finally ours. Literature, the kind you will be reading in this book, provides countless opportunities for meeting and learning new words. Literature, as you have seen, also provides the context for seeing these new words used with precision and effect. As you work through the pages in this book, you will be developing a larger and stronger vocabulary—a storehouse of words that become your tools for learning.

4. Skills transfer. You are using this book to develop your ability to read literature with increased speed and comprehension. With regular practice and a little effort, you will be successful in reaching that goal.

As we mentioned, you will also be improving your context skills and building a bigger vocabulary. These are all wonderful results from using this book.

But, perhaps the greatest benefit of all is the application of these improvements to all of your reading tasks, not just literature. Using this book will make you a better reader, and *better readers read everything better.*

Reading Literature Faster

Through literature we share an experience with a writer. That experience may be presented as a conversation, a character or scene, an emotion, or an event.

Let's examine these four kinds of presentation. Let's see if there are characteristics or clues we can use to help us identify each kind. Once we know what we are expected to experience, we can read more intelligently and more quickly.

When you are working in this book, your instructor will schedule a few moments for you to preview each selection before timing begins. Use the preview time to scan the selection rapidly, looking for one of the following kinds of presentation.

1. Reading and Understanding a Conversation

A conversation is intended to tell us what characters are thinking or feeling—the best way to do this is through their own words.

Read the following conversation between George and his mother, an excerpt from "George's Mother" by Stephen Crane:

> Finally he said savagely: "Damn these early hours!" His mother jumped as if he had thrown a missile at her. "Why, George—" she began.
>
> George broke in again. "Oh, I know all that—but this gettin' up in th' mornin' so early just makes me sick. Jest when a man is gettin' his mornin' nap he's gotta get up. I—"
>
> "George, dear," said his mother, "yeh know I hate yeh to swear, dear. Now, please don't." She looked beseechingly at him.
>
> He made a swift gesture. "Well, I ain't swearin', am I?" he demanded. "I was only sayin' that this gettin'-up business gives me a pain, wasn't I?"
>
> "Well, yeh know how swearin' hurts me," protested the little old woman. She seemed about to sob. She gazed off . . . apparently recalling persons who had never been profane.

First, is this a conversation? Yes, we know it is. There are quotation marks throughout indicating words spoken by the characters. So, to identify a conversation, we look for quotation marks.

Next, does this conversation tell us what the characters are thinking or feeling? It certainly does—this conversation is unmistakably clear. We know how George *feels* about getting up in the morning, and we know how his mother *feels* about profanity.

Finally, how should we read this and other conversations we encounter in literature? Join the conversation; pretend you are one of the speakers and that these are your own words. Listen to the other character as though words are being addressed to you.

Conversations can be read quickly and understood well when you recognize them and become part of them.

2. Reading About and Understanding a Character or Scene

How do we learn about a character? There are many ways. Writers introduce characters (1) by telling us what they look like; (2) by what they say; (3) by the things they do; and (4) by telling us what others think and say about them:

> He was a staid, placid gentleman, something past the prime of life, yet upright in his carriage for all that, and slim as a greyhound. He was well mounted upon a sturdy chestnut cob, and had the graceful seat of an experienced horseman; while his riding gear, though free from such fopperies as were then in vogue, was handsome and well chosen. He wore a riding coat of a somewhat brighter green than might have been expected to suit the taste of a gentleman of his years, with a short, black velvet cape, and laced pocket holes and cuffs, all of a jaunty fashion; his linen too, was of the finest kind, worked in a rich pattern at the wrists and throat, and scrupulously white. Although he seemed, judging from the mud he had picked up on the way, to have come from London, his horse was as smooth and cool as his own iron-gray periwig and pigtail.

Obviously a character is being introduced to us in this passage from *Barnaby Rudge* by Charles Dickens. We are told how he carries himself and how he is dressed. We even know a little about what he has been doing.

The question to ask yourself is: Is this character lifelike and real? Real characters should be like real people—good and bad, happy and sad, alike and different. In reading about characters, look for the same details you look for in all people.

Similarly, when a scene or location is being described, look for words which tell about size, shape, color, appearance. Such descriptor words help us picture in our minds the place being described. Try to visualize the scene as you read.

3. Experiencing an Emotion Through Literature

When a writer presents an emotion for us to experience, the intent is to produce an effect within us. The intended effect may be pity, fear, revulsion, or some other emotion. The writer wants us to *feel* something.

In the following passage from *Jane Eyre* by Charlotte Brontë, what emotions are we expected to feel for the character?

> John had not much affection for his mother and sisters, and an antipathy to me. He bullied and punished me; not two or three times in the week, not once or twice in the day, but continually: every nerve I had feared him, and every morsel of flesh on my bones shrank when he came near. There were moments when I was bewildered by the terror he inspired, because I had no appeal whatever against either his menaces or his inflictions; the servants did not like to offend their young master by taking my part against him, and Mrs. Reed was blind and deaf on the subject: She never saw him strike or heard him abuse me, though he did both now and then in her very presence; more frequently behind her back.

Do you feel sorry for this girl because she is being abused? Do you feel compassion because she is suffering? Are you suffering with her? Do you feel anger toward her abuser? What other effects are intended? How are these effects produced?

Emotional and provocative words and expressions have been employed by the writer to paint a vivid portrait of her character's predicament. Can you identify some of the words? What did John do? He *bullied, struck, punished,* and *abused.* The girl felt fear, bewilderment, and terror. These very expressive and emotional words and phrases are the clues provided by the writer to help her readers read and comprehend effectively.

4. Reading About and Understanding an Event

In describing an event—a series of actions—the writer is telling us a story, and the elements of the story are presented in some kind of order or pattern. Read this passage from *Around the World in Eighty Days* by Jules Verne:

> Mr. Fogg and his two companions took their places on a bench opposite the desks of the magistrate and his clerk. Immediately after, Judge Obadiah, a fat, round man, followed by the clerk, entered. He proceeded to take down a wig which was hanging on a nail, and put it hurriedly on his head.
>
> "The first case," said he. Then, putting his hand to his head, he exclaimed "Heh! This is not my wig!"
>
> "No, your worship," returned the clerk, "it is mine."
>
> "My dear Mr. Oysterpuff, how can a judge give a wise sentence in a clerk's wig?"
>
> The wigs were exchanged.

Did you see how this little story was told? The events in the story were presented in chronological order—from first to last as they occurred. This is a frequently used and easily recognized pattern, but not the only one writers use. The story could have been told in reverse—the story could have opened with the judge wearing the wrong wig and then gone on to explain how the mistake happened.

In passages like these, look for the events in the story and see how they are related, how one event follows or builds on the other. By recognizing the pattern of storytelling and using the pattern as an aid to organizing and understanding the events, you can become a better and faster reader.

How to Use This Book

1 **Read the lessons**
First, read the lessons on pages 8 through 11. These lessons teach you how to recognize and identify the kinds of presentation you encounter in literature and in the selections in this book.

2 **Preview**
Find a literature selection to read and wait for your instructor's signal to preview. You will have 30 seconds to preview (scan) the selection to identify the author's kind of presentation.

3 **Begin reading**
When your instructor gives you the signal, begin reading. Read at a slightly faster-than-normal speed. Read well enough so that you will be able to answer questions about what you have read.

7 **Fill in the progress graph**
Enter your score and plot your reading time on the graph on page 118 or 119. The right-hand side of the graph shows your words-per-minute reading speed. Write this number at the bottom of the page on the line labeled *Words per Minute.*

"Quick, Huck, snatch on your clothes—I've got it! Bloodhound!"

In two minutes we was tearing up the river road in the dark towards the village. Old Jeff Hooker had a bloodhound, and Tom was going to borrow it. I says.

"The trail's too old. Tom—and besides, it's rained, you know."

"It don't make any difference, Huck. If the body's hid in the woods anywhere around the hound will find it. If he's been murdered and buried, they wouldn't bury him deep, it ain't likely, and if the dog goes over the spot he'll scent him, sure. Huck, we're going to be celebrated, sure as you're born!"

He was just a-blazing; and whenever he got afire he was most likely to get afire all over. That was the way this time. In two minutes he had got it all ciphered out, and wasn't only just going to find the corpse—no, he was going to get on the track of that murderer and hunt him down, too; and not only that, but he was going to stick to him till—

"Well," I says, "you better find the corpse first. I reckon that's a-plenty for today. For all we know, there ain't any corpse and nobody ain't been murdered. That cuss could 'a' gone off somers and not been killed at all."

That graveled him, and he says:

"Huck Finn, I never see such a person as you to want to spoil everything. As long as you can't see anything hopeful in a thing, you won't let anybody else. What good can it do you to throw cold water on that corpse and get up that selfish theory that there ain't been any murder? None in the world. I don't see how you can act so. I wouldn't treat you like that, and you know it. Here we've got a noble good opportunity to make a reputation, and—"

"Oh, go ahead," I says. "I'm sorry, and I take it all back. I didn't mean nothing. Fix it any way you want it. He ain't any consequence to me. If he's killed, I'm as glad of it as you are, and if he—"

"I never said anything about being glad; I only—"

"Well, then, I'm as sorry as you are. Any way you druther have it, that is the way I druther have it. He—"

"There ain't any druthers about it."

Reading Time :40   Comprehension Score _____   Words per Minute _____   127

Recalling Facts

1. Tom wanted to borrow Jeff Hooker's
   - a. rifle.
   - b. map.
   - c. bloodhound.

2. Tom and Huck were looking for a
   - a. treasure.
   - b. dead body.
   - c. cave.

3. Tom was hoping to
   - a. become famous.
   - b. get a reward.
   - c. avoid trouble.

4. The boy most excited about the plan was
   - a. Tom.
   - b. Huck.
   - c. Jeff.

5. Huck wasn't really sure there was a
   - a. robbery.
   - b. fire.
   - c. murder.

Understanding the Passage

6. Old Jeff Hooker lived in the
   - a. woods.
   - b. village.
   - c. city.

7. Tom was very
   - a. sure of himself.
   - b. uncertain.
   - c. frightened.

8. Tom was
   - a. working for the sheriff.
   - b. looking for adventure.
   - c. trying to help the accused murderer.

9. Tom got upset with
   - a. Jeff.
   - b. his mother.
   - c. Huck.

10. Huck became very
    - a. apologetic.
    - b. angry.
    - c. shy.

128

Recalling Facts

1. Tom wanted to borrow Jeff Hooker's
   - a. woods.
   - b. village.
   - c. bloodhound.

2. Tom and Huck were looking for a
   - a. treasure.
   - b. dead body.
   - c. cave.

Understanding the Passage

6. Old Jeff Hooker lived in the
   - a. woods.
   - b. village.
   - c. city.

7. Tom was very
   - a. sure of himself.
   - b. uncertain.
   - c. frightened.

Reading Time :40   Comprehension Score 90   Words per Minute _____   127

---

4 Record your time

When you finish reading, look at the blackboard and note your reading time. Your reading time will be the lowest time remaining on the board, or the next number to be erased. Write this time at the bottom of the page on the line labeled *Reading Time.*

5 Answer the questions

Answer the ten questions on the next page. There are five fact questions and five thought questions. Pick the *best* answer to each question and put an x in the box beside it.

6 Correct your answers

Using the Answer Key on pages 116 and 117, correct your work. Circle your wrong answers and put an x in the box you should have marked. Score 10 points for each correct answer. Write your score at the bottom of the page on the line labeled *Comprehension Score.*

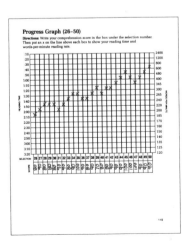

Progress Graph (26–50)

Directions: Write your comprehension score in the box under the selection number. Then put an x on the line above each box to show your reading time and words-per-minute reading rate.

119

13

Instructions for the Pacing Drills

From time to time your instructor may wish to conduct pacing drills using *Timed Readings*. For this work you need to use the Pacing Dots printed in the margins of your book pages. The dots will help you regulate your reading speed to match the pace set by your instructor or announced on the reading cassette tape.

Pacing Dots

You will be reading at the correct pace if you are at the dot when your instructor says "Mark" or when you hear a tone on the tape. If you are ahead of the pace, read a little more slowly; if you are behind the pace, increase your reading speed. Try to match the pace exactly.

Follow these steps.

Step 1: Record the pace. At the bottom of the page, write on the line labeled *Words per Minute* the rate announced by the instructor or by the speaker on the tape.

Step 2: Begin reading. Wait for the signal to begin reading. Read at a slightly faster-than-normal speed. You will not know how on-target your pace is until you hear your instructor say "Mark" or until you hear the first tone on the tape. After a little practice you will be able to select an appropriate starting speed most of the time.

Step 3: Adjust your pace. As you read, try to match the pace set by the instructor or the tape. Read more slowly or more quickly as necessary. You should be reading the line beside the dot when you hear the pacing signal. The pacing sounds may distract you at first. Don't worry about it. Keep reading and your concentration will return.

Step 4: Stop and answer questions. Stop reading when you are told to, even if you have not finished the selection. Answer the questions right away. Correct your work and record your score on the line *Comprehension Score*. Strive to maintain 80 percent comprehension on each drill as you gradually increase your pace.

Step 5: Fill in the pacing graph. Transfer your words-per-minute rate to the box labeled *Pace* on the pacing graph on page 120. Then plot your comprehension score on the line above the box.

These pacing drills are designed to help you become a more flexible reader. They encourage you to "break out" of a pattern of reading everything at the same speed.

The drills help in other ways, too. Sometimes in a reading program you reach a certain level and bog down. You don't seem able to move on and progress. The pacing drills will help you to work your way out of such slumps and get your reading program moving again.

It might have been half an hour before each individual, including even the women and children, was in his place. The delay had been created by the grave preparations that were deemed necessary to so solemn and unusual a conference. But when the sun was seen climbing above the tops of that mountain against whose bosom the Delaware Indians had constructed their encampment, most were seated; and as his bright rays darted from behind the outline of trees that fringed the eminence, they fell upon as grave, as attentive, and as deeply interested a multitude, as was probably ever before lighted by his morning beams. Its number somewhat exceeded a thousand souls.

In a collection of such serious savages, there is never to be found any impatient aspirant after premature distinction, standing ready to move his auditors to some hasty, and, perhaps, injudicious discussion, in order that his own reputation may be the gainer. An act of so much precipitancy and presumption would seal the downfall of precocious intellect forever. It rested solely with the oldest and most experienced of the men to lay the subject of the conference before the people. Until such a one chose to make some movement, no deeds in arms, no natural gifts, nor any renown as an orator, would have justified the slightest interruption. On the present occasion, the aged warrior whose privilege it was to speak, was silent, seemingly oppressed with the magnitude of his subject. The delay had already continued long beyond the usual deliberative pause that always precedes a conference. Still, no sign of impatience or surprise escaped even the youngest boy. Occasionally, an eye was raised from the earth, where the looks of most were riveted, and strayed towards a particular lodge, that was, however, in no manner distinguished from those around it, except in the peculiar care that had been taken to protect it against the assaults of the weather.

At length, one of those low murmurs that are so apt to disturb a multitude, was heard, and the whole nation arose to their feet by a common impulse. At that the door of the lodge in question opened, and three men, issuing from it, slowly approached the place of consultation. They were all aged, even beyond that period to which the oldest present had reached; but one in the center, who leaned on his companions for support, was especially ancient.

Recalling Facts

1. The number of people at the
   conference was roughly
   □ a. one hundred.
   □ b. five hundred.
   □ c. one thousand.

2. The Indians' conferences
   were run by the
   □ a. greatest orators in
      the tribe.
   □ b. oldest and most
      experienced members
      of the tribe.
   □ c. warriors with precocious
      intellect.

3. On this particular occasion,
   the delay was
   □ a. caused by bad weather.
   □ b. longer than usual.
   □ c. making people nervous.

4. Most of the people present
   kept their eyes fixed on the
   □ a. ground.
   □ b. horizon.
   □ c. lodges.

5. When the oldest Indian
   appeared, he was
   □ a. leaning on his
      companions for support.
   □ b. wearing an elaborate
      warrior's costume.
   □ c. both a and b.

Understanding the Passage

6. The people gathered for the
   conference in the
   □ a. early morning.
   □ b. middle of the day.
   □ c. late afternoon.

7. The Indians considered this
   conference to be a
   □ a. joyous occasion.
   □ b. serious occasion.
   □ c. fatal occasion.

8. The young Indians were very
   □ a. impatient for the
      conference to begin.
   □ b. angry that they
      could not attend
      the conference.
   □ c. respectful of
      their elders.

9. Women never
   □ a. attended conferences.
   □ b. presided over
      conferences.
   □ c. brought their childen
      to conferences.

10. Apparently, the three men
    who emerged from the lodge
    □ a. were going to lead the
       tribal conference.
    □ b. could not find the
       ancient leader of
       the tribe.
    □ c. wanted the people to
       wait a little longer.

from **The Tenant of Wildfell Hall** *by Anne Brontë*

You must go back with me to the autumn of 1827.

My father, as you know, was a sort of gentleman farmer; and I, by his express desire, succeeded him in the same quiet occupation, not very willingly, for ambition urged me to higher aims, and self-conceit assured me that, in disregarding its voice, I was burying my talent in the earth, and hiding my light under a bushel. My mother had done her utmost to persuade me that I was capable of great achievements, but my father, who thought ambition was the surest road to ruin, and change but another word for destruction, would listen to no scheme for bettering either my own condition, or that of my fellow mortals. He assured me it was all rubbish, and exhorted me, with his dying breath, to continue in the good old way, to follow his steps, and those of his father before him, and let my highest ambition be to walk honestly through the world, looking neither to the right hand nor to the left, and to transmit the paternal acres to my children in, at least, as flourishing a condition as he left them to me.

"Well! An honest and industrious farmer is one of the most useful members of society, and if I devote my talents to the cultivation of my farm, and the improvement of agriculture in general, I shall thereby benefit, not only my own immediate connections and dependents, but, in some degree, mankind at large—hence I shall not have lived in vain."

With such reflections as these I was endeavoring to console myself, as I plodded home from the fields, one cold, damp, cloudy evening towards the close of October. But the gleam of a bright red fire through the parlor window had more effect in cheering my spirits, and rebuking my thankless repinings, than all the sage reflections and good resolutions I had forced my mind to frame; for I was young then, remember—only four-and-twenty—and had not acquired half the rule over my own spirit that I now possess—trifling as that may be.

However, that haven of bliss must not be entered till I had exchanged my miry boots for a clean pair of shoes, and my rough surtout for a respectable coat, and made myself generally presentable before decent society, for my mother was vastly particular on certain points.

Recalling Facts

1. The narrator's father was a
   - ☐ a. preacher.
   - ☐ b. schoolteacher.
   - ☐ c. gentleman farmer.

2. The narrator's mother believed her son was
   - ☐ a. capable of great things.
   - ☐ b. lazy and stupid.
   - ☐ c. born to be a farmer.

3. The narrator's father wanted his son to become a
   - ☐ a. businessman.
   - ☐ b. salesman.
   - ☐ c. farmer.

4. The sight of a bright red fire in the fireplace
   - ☐ a. cheered the narrator.
   - ☐ b. frightened the narrator.
   - ☐ c. depressed the narrator.

5. Before entering the house, the narrator had to
   - ☐ a. ring the doorbell.
   - ☐ b. feed the chickens.
   - ☐ c. take off his boots.

Understanding the Passage

6. The narrator did not believe
   - ☐ a. farmers were honest people.
   - ☐ b. he was meant to be a farmer.
   - ☐ c. his mother loved him.

7. The narrator reluctantly
   - ☐ a. honored his father's wishes.
   - ☐ b. entered politics.
   - ☐ c. bade farewell to his family.

8. The narrator's mother had
   - ☐ a. certain strict rules.
   - ☐ b. an incurable illness.
   - ☐ c. plans to remarry.

9. At the age of twenty-four, the narrator was
   - ☐ a. drafted into the army.
   - ☐ b. the father of three children.
   - ☐ c. still living with his mother.

10. The narrator's father did not like
    - ☐ a. the country life.
    - ☐ b. innovation.
    - ☐ c. his neighbors.

3 *from* Sherlock Holmes and The Adventure of the Devil's Foot *by Arthur Conan Doyle*

In the spring of the year 1897, Sherlock Holmes's iron constitution showed some symptoms of giving way in the face of constant hard work of a most exacting kind, aggravated, perhaps, by occasional indiscretions of his own. In March of that year Dr. Moore Agar, of Harley Street, whose dramatic introduction to Holmes I may someday recount, gave positive injunctions that the famous private agent lay aside all his cases and surrender himself to complete rest if he wished to avert an absolute breakdown. The state of his health was not a matter in which he himself took the faintest interest, for his mental detachment was absolute, but he was induced at last, on the threat of being permanently disqualified from work, to give himself a complete change of scene and air. Thus it was that in the early spring of that year we found ourselves together in a small cottage near Poldhu Bay, at the further extremity of the Cornish peninsula.

It was a singular spot, and one peculiarly well suited to the grim humor of my patient. From the windows of our little whitewashed house, we looked down upon the whole sinister semicircle of Mounts Bay, that old death trap of sailing vessels, with its fringe of black cliffs and surge-swept reefs on which innumerable seamen have met their end. With a northerly breeze it lies placid and sheltered, inviting the storm-tossed craft to tack into it for rest and protection.

Then come the sudden swirl round of the wind, the blustering gale from the southwest, the dragging anchor, the lee shore, and the last battle in the creaming breakers. The wise mariner stands far out from that evil place.

On the land side our surroundings were as somber as on the sea. It was a country of rolling moors, lonely and dun colored, with an occasional church tower to mark the site of some old world village. In every direction upon these moors there were traces of some vanished race which had passed utterly away, and left as its sole record strange monuments of stone, irregular mounds which contained the burned ashes of the dead, and curious earthworks which hinted at prehistoric strife. The glamour and mystery of the place, with its sinister atmosphere of forgotten nations, appealed to the imagination of my friend, and he spent much of his time in long walks and solitary meditations upon the moor.

Recalling Facts

1. Dr. Moore Agar wanted Holmes to
   - ☐ a. solve a murder.
   - ☐ b. take a long rest.
   - ☐ c. meet him on the Cornish peninsula.

2. Holmes was not particularly interested in
   - ☐ a. the arts.
   - ☐ b. the narrator's health.
   - ☐ c. his own health.

3. In the spring of 1897, Holmes went to
   - ☐ a. the Scottish highlands.
   - ☐ b. Poldhu Bay.
   - ☐ c. the Cliffs of Dover.

4. The narrator and Holmes stayed in a
   - ☐ a. small cottage.
   - ☐ b. local hotel.
   - ☐ c. friend's home.

5. Some vanished race left behind
   - ☐ a. church towers.
   - ☐ b. stone monuments.
   - ☐ c. cave paintings.

Understanding the Passage

6. Holmes apparently had
   - ☐ a. previously enjoyed good health.
   - ☐ b. been sickly for years.
   - ☐ c. never liked doctors.

7. Holmes was a man who
   - ☐ a. liked hard work and challenge.
   - ☐ b. lacked common sense.
   - ☐ c. refused to listen to any physician.

8. The idea of taking a vacation
   - ☐ a. did not please Holmes.
   - ☐ b. disappointed Holmes's clients.
   - ☐ c. both a and b.

9. Mounts Bay
   - ☐ a. had some fabulous beaches.
   - ☐ b. was a dangerous place for sailors.
   - ☐ c. was too shallow for most boats.

10. The moors
   - ☐ a. seemed to catch Holmes's interest.
   - ☐ b. were too lonely for Holmes.
   - ☐ c. were often crowded with tourists.

For some days, nothing was seen and little was heard of the "dear sufferers," as the old ladies called them. But they were not forgotten; the first words uttered when any of the young people met were: "How is Jack?" "Seen Jill yet?" and all waited with impatience for the moment when they could be admitted to their favorite mates, more than ever objects of interest now.

Meantime, the captives spent the first few days in sleep, pain, and trying to accept the hard fact that school and play were over for months perhaps. But young spirits are wonderfully elastic and soon cheer up, and healthy young bodies heal fast, or easily adapt themselves to new conditions. So our invalids began to mend on the fourth day, and to drive their nurses to distraction with efforts to amuse them, before the first week was over.

The most successful attempt originated in Ward No. 1, as Mrs. Minot called Jack's apartment, and we will give our sympathizing readers some idea of this place, which became the stage whereon were enacted many varied and remarkable scenes.

Each of the Minot boys had his own room, and there collected his own treasures and trophies, arranged to suit his convenience and taste. Frank's was full of books, maps, machinery, chemical messes, and geometrical drawings, which adorned the walls like intricate cobwebs. A big chair, where he read and studied with his heels higher than his head, a basket of apples for refreshment at all hours of the day, and an immense inkstand, in which several pens were always apparently bathing their feet, were the principal ornaments of his scholastic retreat.

Jack's hobby was athletic sports, for he was bent on having a strong and active body for his happy little soul to live and enjoy itself in. So a severe simplicity reigned in his apartment; in summer, especially, for then his floor was bare, his windows were uncurtained, and the chairs uncushioned, the bed being as narrow and hard as Napoleon's. The only ornaments were dumbbells, whips, bats, rods, skates, boxing gloves, a big bath pan, and a small library, consisting chiefly of books on games, horses, health, hunting, and travels. In winter his mother made things more comfortable by introducing rugs, curtains, and a fire. Jack, also, relented slightly in the severity of his training, occasionally indulging in the national buckwheat cake, instead of the prescribed oatmeal porridge.

Recalling Facts

1. The "dear sufferers" referred to
   - ☐ a. the old ladies.
   - ☐ b. Jack and Jill.
   - ☐ c. Mr. and Mrs. Minot.

2. The invalids began to mend
   - ☐ a. immediately.
   - ☐ b. on the fourth day.
   - ☐ c. after the first week.

3. Ward No. 1 was where
   - ☐ a. Jill stayed.
   - ☐ b. Jack stayed.
   - ☐ c. the nurses slept.

4. Frank's room was filled with
   - ☐ a. books and maps.
   - ☐ b. bats and gloves.
   - ☐ c. magazines and comic books.

5. Jack's room was
   - ☐ a. adorned with all kinds of drawings.
   - ☐ b. equipped for a serious scholar.
   - ☐ c. kept as simple as possible.

Understanding the Passage

6. Jack and Jill
   - ☐ a. had many friends.
   - ☐ b. lacked proper medical care.
   - ☐ c. were working on geometry.

7. Jack and Jill
   - ☐ a. remained depressed.
   - ☐ b. fought with each other.
   - ☐ c. accepted their fate.

8. Frank appeared to be
   - ☐ a. an athlete.
   - ☐ b. a scholar.
   - ☐ c. a troublemaker.

9. Jack was most concerned with developing a
   - ☐ a. firm knowledge of geometry.
   - ☐ b. healthy body.
   - ☐ c. beautifully decorated room.

10. Jack's room evidently had
    - ☐ a. a fireplace.
    - ☐ b. an immense inkstand.
    - ☐ c. two beds.

As Queequeg and I are now fairly embarked in this business of whaling; and as this business of whaling has somehow to be regarded among landsmen as a rather unpoetical and disreputable pursuit; therefore, I am all anxiety to convince ye, ye landsmen, of the injustice hereby done to us hunters of whales.

Among people at large, the business of whaling is not accounted on a level with what are called the liberal professions. If a stranger were introduced into any miscellaneous company as a harpooner, say; and if in imitation of the naval officers he should append the initials S. W. F. (Sperm Whale Fishery) to his visiting card, such a procedure would be deemed ridiculous.

Doubtless one leading reason why the world declines honoring us whalemen is this: they think that, at best, our vocation is a butchering sort of business; and that when actively engaged therein, we are surrounded by all manner of filth. Butchers we are, that is true. But butchers, also, have been all military commanders, whom the world invariably delights to honor. And as for the matter of the alleged uncleanliness of our business, ye shall soon be initiated into certain facts which will triumphantly plant the sperm whaleship at least among the cleanliest things of this tidy earth.

But even granting the charge in question to be true, what disordered slippery decks of a whaleship are comparable to the unspeakable carrion of those battlefields from which so many soldiers return to drink in all ladies' praises? And if the idea of peril so much glorifies the popular notion of the soldier's profession, let me assure ye that many a veteran who has freely marched up to a battery of canon would quickly recoil at the sight of the sperm whale's vast tail, fanning into eddies the air over his head. For what are the comprehensible terrors of man compared with the interlinked terrors and wonders of God!

No honor in whaling? Drive down your hat in presence of the Czar, and take it off to Queequeg! I know a man that in his lifetime has taken three hundred and fifty whales. I account that man more honorable than that great captain of antiquity who boasted of taking as many walled towns.

For many years past the whaleship has been the pioneer in ferreting out the remotest and least known parts of the earth.

Reading Time _____   *Comprehension Score* _____   *Words per Minute* _____   23

Recalling Facts

1. The narrator refers to people who criticize whaling as
   - ☐ a. landlubbers.
   - ☐ b. hunters.
   - ☐ c. landsmen.

2. The narrator agrees that whalemen are
   - ☐ a. uncaring.
   - ☐ b. unworthy of respect.
   - ☐ c. butchers.

3. According to the narrator, the sperm whaleship is a
   - ☐ a. bloody thing.
   - ☐ b. clean thing.
   - ☐ c. disgraceful thing.

4. The narrator states that people interested in honor should take their hats off to
   - ☐ a. the whales.
   - ☐ b. Queequeg.
   - ☐ c. the narrator.

5. The narrator knew a man who
   - ☐ a. took 350 whales.
   - ☐ b. took 350 walled cities.
   - ☐ c. sailed on 350 warships.

Understanding the Passage

6. Most people regarded whaling as
   - ☐ a. disgusting and disagreeable work.
   - ☐ b. a noble occupation.
   - ☐ c. equal to waging war.

7. People honor soldiers in part because soldiers
   - ☐ a. perform violent deeds.
   - ☐ b. know how to kill.
   - ☐ c. face great danger.

8. The narrator has little good to say about
   - ☐ a. the military.
   - ☐ b. whaleships.
   - ☐ c. Queequeg.

9. One of the most frightening aspects of whaling is
   - ☐ a. cleaning a dead whale.
   - ☐ b. slipping on whale blubber.
   - ☐ c. seeing the tail of an angry whale.

10. The narrator suggests that one service whalemen perform is
    - ☐ a. controlling drunkards and criminals.
    - ☐ b. providing fuel oil for lamps.
    - ☐ c. the exploration of uncharted waters.

The young lady who took Ormond's fancy was one of the remarkably pleasant, sprightly, clever, most agreeable Miss Lardners. She did not interest him much, but she amused him exceedingly. Her sister had once advised her, "Anne, you can't be pretty, so you had better be odd." Anne took the advice, set up for being odd, and succeeded. She was a mimic, a wit, and very satirical; and as long as the satire touched only those for whom he did not care, Ormond was extremely diverted. He didn't think it quite feminine or amiable, but still it was entertaining: there was also something flattering in being exempted from this general reprobation and ridicule. Miss Lardner was intolerant of all insipid people—*flats*, as she called them. How far Ormond might have been drawn on by this laughing, talking, satirical, flattering wit, there is no saying; but luckily they fell out one evening about Old Lady Annaly. Miss Lardner wasn't aware that Ormond knew, much less could she have conceived, that he liked her ladyship. Miss Lardner was mimicking her for the amusement of a set of young ladies, when Harry Ormond came in: he was not as much diverted as she expected.

"Mr. Ormond doesn't know the *original*—the copy is lost upon him," said Miss Lardner; "and happy it is for you," continued she turning to him, "that you do not know her, for Lady Annaly is as stiff and tiresome an original as ever there was—and the worst of it is, she is an original without originality."

"Lady Annaly!" exclaimed Ormond, with surprise, "surely not the Lady Annaly I know."

"Oh, I beg your pardon, Mr. Ormond, if she is a friend of yours—I humbly beg your forgiveness—I did not know your taste was so *very good!* Lady Annaly is a fine old lady, certainly—vastly respectable; and I so far agree with Mr. Ormond, that of the two paragons, mother and daughter, I prefer the mother. Paragons in their teens are insufferable: patterns of perfection are good for nothing in society, except to be torn to pieces."

Miss Lardner pursued this diversion of tearing them to pieces, still flattering herself that her present wit and drollery would prevail with Ormond, as she had found it prevail with most people against an absent friend, but Ormond thought upon this occasion she showed more flippancy than wit.

Recalling Facts

1. Anne Lardner's sister had told her that she could never be
   - ☐ a. clever.
   - ☐ b. married.
   - ☐ c. pretty.

2. Miss Lardner called insipid people
   - ☐ a. paragons.
   - ☐ b. flats.
   - ☐ c. drones.

3. Miss Lardner amused Ormond by
   - ☐ a. arranging parlor games.
   - ☐ b. mimicking people.
   - ☐ c. reciting poetry.

4. Miss Lardner did not know that Ormond
   - ☐ a. disliked satire.
   - ☐ b. liked Lady Annaly.
   - ☐ c. wanted to marry her.

5. Ormond and Miss Lardner fell out because of a disagreement about
   - ☐ a. Anne's sister.
   - ☐ b. Lady Annaly's daughter.
   - ☐ c. Lady Annaly.

Understanding the Passage

6. When Ormond heard Miss Lardner attacking Lady Annaly he was
   - ☐ a. amused.
   - ☐ b. annoyed.
   - ☐ c. unconvinced.

7. Ormond felt lucky to be
   - ☐ a. spared from Miss Lardner's sharp satire.
   - ☐ b. engaged to Anne Lardner.
   - ☐ c. introduced to Anne Lardner's sister.

8. Miss Lardner was surprised to hear that Ormond
   - ☐ a. knew Lady Annaly.
   - ☐ b. was in love with Lady Annaly's daughter.
   - ☐ c. was related to Lady Annaly.

9. Miss Lardner considered Lady Annaly to be
   - ☐ a. dull.
   - ☐ b. witty.
   - ☐ c. intimidating.

10. The narrator viewed Ormond and Miss Lardner's disagreement with
    - ☐ a. sorrow.
    - ☐ b. relief.
    - ☐ c. disapproval.

from **Rob Roy** *by Sir Walter Scott*

I had indirectly gained from Andrews an important piece of information, that Father Vaughan, namely, was not supposed to be at the Hall. If, therefore, there appeared light in the windows of the library this evening, it either could not be his, or he was observing a very secret and suspicious line of conduct. I waited with impatience the time of sunset and of twilight, and it had hardly arrived, when a gleam from the windows of the library was seen, dimly distinguishable amidst the still enduring light of the evening. I marked its first glimpse, however, as speedily as the benighted sailor descries the first distant twinkle of the lighthouse which marks his course. The feelings of doubt and propriety, which had hitherto contended with my curiosity and jealousy, vanished when an opportunity of gratifying the former was presented to me. I reentered the house, and, avoiding the more frequented apartments with the consciousness of one who wishes to keep his purpose secret, I reached the door of the library—hesitated for a moment as my hand was upon the latch—heard a suppressed step within—opened the door—and found Miss Vernon alone.

Diana appeared surprised, whether at my sudden entrance, or from some other cause, I could not guess; but there was in her appearance a degree of flutter, which I had never before remarked, and which I knew could only be produced by unusual emotion. Yet she was calm in a moment; and such is the force of conscience, that I, who studied to surprise her, seemed myself the surprised, and was certainly the embarrassed person.

"Has anything happened?" said Miss Vernon. "Has anyone arrived at the Hall?"

"No one that I know of," I answered, in some confusion; "I only sought the Orlando."

"It lies there," said Miss Vernon, pointing to the table.

In removing one or two books to get at that which I pretended to seek, I was, in truth, meditating to make a handsome retreat from an investigation to which I felt my assurance inadequate, when I perceived a man's glove lying upon the table. My eyes encountered those of Miss Vernon, who blushed deeply.

"It is one of my relics," she said with hesitation, replying not to my words, but to my looks; "it is one of the gloves of my grandfather, the original of the superb Vandyke which you admire."

Recalling Facts

1. The narrator had learned that
   Father Vaughan was not
   supposed to
   □ a. be in the Hall.
   □ b. read the Orlando.
   □ c. talk to Miss Vernon.

2. The narrator sneaked through
   the house and opened the
   door of the
   □ a. dining room.
   □ b. library.
   □ c. kitchen.

3. Inside, the narrator found
   □ a. no one.
   □ b. Miss Vernon alone.
   □ c. Miss Vernon and a
   companion.

4. The narrator said that he was
   looking for
   □ a. Diana.
   □ b. the Orlando.
   □ c. Father Vaughan.

5. Miss Vernon said that the
   glove belonged to her
   □ a. grandfather.
   □ b. servant.
   □ c. son.

Understanding the Passage

6. The narrator was very
   anxious to see
   □ a. whether Miss Vernon
   had left the Hall.
   □ b. if the Orlando had
   been stolen.
   □ c. if there would be a light
   in the window.

7. The narrator was most
   motivated by his
   □ a. curiosity.
   □ b. doubt.
   □ c. jealousy.

8. While moving through the
   house, the narrator
   □ a. did not want to be seen.
   □ b. called out for
   Miss Vernon.
   □ c. stopped to question
   the residents.

9. Within moments of seeing
   the narrator, Miss Vernon
   □ a. screamed for help.
   □ b. bitterly denounced
   his trickery.
   □ c. regained her composure.

10. After encountering Miss Vernon,
    the narrator wanted to
    □ a. study the Orlando
    in detail.
    □ b. investigate the owner-
    ship of the Vandyke.
    □ c. leave as graciously
    as possible.

from **Esther: An American Novel** *by Henry Adams*

The new church of St. John's, on Fifth Avenue, was thronged the morning of the last Sunday of October, in the year 1880. Sitting in the gallery, beneath the unfinished frescoes, and looking down the nave, one caught an effect of autumn gardens, a suggestion of chrysanthemums and geraniums, or of October woods, dashed with scarlet oaks and yellow maples. As a display of austerity the show was a failure, but if cheerful content and innocent adornment please the Author of the lilies and roses, there was reason to hope that this first service at St. John's found favor in His sight, ●
even though it showed no victory over the world or the flesh in this part of the United States. The sun came in through the figure of St. John in his crimson and green garments of glass, and scattered more color where colors already rivaled the flowers of a prize show; while huge prophets and evangelists in flowing robes looked down from the red walls on a display of human vanities that would have called out a vehement Lamentation of Jeremiah or Song of Solomon, had these poets been present in flesh as they were in figure.

Solomon was a brilliant but not an accurate observer; he looked at the ●
world from the narrow standpoint of his own temple. Here in New York he could not have truthfully said that all was vanity, for even a more ill-natured satirist than he must have confessed that there was in this new temple today a perceptible interest in religion. One might almost have said that religion seemed to be a matter of concern. The audience wore a look of interest, and, even after their first gaze of admiration and whispered criticism at the splendors of their new church, when at length the clergy- ●
man entered to begin the service, a ripple of excitement swept across the field of bonnets until there was almost a murmur as of rustling cornfields within the many colored walls of St. John's.

In a remote pew, hidden under a gallery of the transept, two persons looked on with especial interest. The number of strangers who crowded in after them forced them to sit closely together, and their low whispers of comment were unheard by their neighbors. Before the service began they talked in a secular tone.

"Wharton's window is too high-toned," said the man.

Recalling Facts

1. The frescoes of St. John's were
   - ☐ a. splendid.
   - ☐ b. too austere.
   - ☐ c. unfinished.

2. The glass figure of
   St. John was
   - ☐ a. red and blue.
   - ☐ b. crimson and green.
   - ☐ c. yellow and white.

3. The brilliant but inaccurate
   observer was
   - ☐ a. Solomon.
   - ☐ b. Jeremiah.
   - ☐ c. St. John.

4. This new church was
   located in
   - ☐ a. Chicago.
   - ☐ b. New York.
   - ☐ c. Boston.

5. The man said that Wharton's
   window was
   - ☐ a. too large.
   - ☐ b. the wrong color.
   - ☐ c. too high-toned.

Understanding the Passage

6. "The Author of the lilies and
   roses" refers to
   - ☐ a. St. John.
   - ☐ b. God.
   - ☐ c. the United States.

7. The figure of St. John was
   part of a
   - ☐ a. painting.
   - ☐ b. statue.
   - ☐ c. stained glass window.

8. The first service at
   St. John's was
   - ☐ a. an extremely
     colorful affair.
   - ☐ b. simple and direct.
   - ☐ c. postponed several
     times.

9. The parishioners could best
   be described as
   - ☐ a. vain but with some
     religious intent.
   - ☐ b. materialistic and
     boldly secular.
   - ☐ c. poor and deeply
     religious.

10. Before the service began, the
    parishioners were most
    interested in
    - ☐ a. their own private
      thoughts and prayers.
    - ☐ b. guessing who would
      give the sermon.
    - ☐ c. the structure and design
      of the church.

Undine lay silent, her hands clasped behind her head. She was plunged in one of the moods of bitter retrospection when all her past seemed like a long struggle for something she could not have, from a trip to Europe to an opera box; and when she felt sure that, as the past had been, so the future would be. And yet, all she sought for was improvement: she honestly wanted the best.

Her first struggle—after she had ceased to scream for candy, or sulk for a new toy—had been to get away from Apex in summer. Her summers, as she looked back on them, seemed to typify all that was dreariest and most exasperating in her life. The earliest had been spent in the yellow "frame" cottage where she had hung on the fence, kicking her toes against the broken palings and exchanging moist chewing gum and half-eaten apples with Indiana Frush. Later on, she had returned from her boarding school to the comparative gentility of summer vacations at the Mealey House, whither her parents, forsaking their squalid suburb, had moved in the first flush of their rising fortunes. The tessellated floors, the plush parlors and organlike radiators of the Mealey House had, aside from their intrinsic elegance, the immense advantage of lifting the Spraggs high above the Frusks, and making it possible for Undine, when she met Indiana in the street, to chill her advances by a careless allusion to the splendors of hotel life. But even in such a setting, and in spite of the social superiority it implied, the long months of the middle western summer, fly-blown, torrid, exhaling stale odors, soon became as insufferable as they had been in the little yellow house.

At school Undine met other girls whose parents took them to the Great Lakes for August; some even went to California, others—oh bliss ineffable! —went "east."

Pale and listless under the stifling boredom of the Mealey House routine, Undine secretly sucked lemons, nibbled slate pencils and drank pints of bitter coffee to aggravate her look of ill-health; and when she learned that even Indiana Frusk was going on a month's visit to Buffalo it needed no artificial aids to emphasize the ravages of envy. Her parents, alarmed by her appearance, were at last convinced of the necessity of change, and timidly, tentatively, they transferred themselves for a month to a staring hotel on a glaring lake.

Recalling Facts

1. Undine had wanted very much to
   - ☐ a. get out of Apex for the summer.
   - ☐ b. enjoy a quiet summer at home.
   - ☐ c. spend the summer with Indiana.

2. When the Spraggs had enough money, they moved
   - ☐ a. into a yellow cottage.
   - ☐ b. to Indiana.
   - ☐ c. into the Mealey House.

3. Undine went to
   - ☐ a. college.
   - ☐ b. public school.
   - ☐ c. boarding school.

4. Undine was jealous when she learned that Indiana Frusk was going to visit
   - ☐ a. Buffalo.
   - ☐ b. California.
   - ☐ c. the Great Lakes.

5. To make herself look sickly, Undine
   - ☐ a. sucked lemons.
   - ☐ b. stopped washing her hair.
   - ☐ c. slept on the floor.

Understanding the Passage

6. Undine was filled with
   - ☐ a. gratitude.
   - ☐ b. intellectual curiosity.
   - ☐ c. unfulfilled passions.

7. Undine's parents
   - ☐ a. were very poor.
   - ☐ b. invested money in the hotel business.
   - ☐ c. had improved their financial situation.

8. Undine liked to
   - ☐ a. flaunt her family's superiority in front of Indiana.
   - ☐ b. vacation in the little yellow cottage.
   - ☐ c. listen to the travel stories of her classmates.

9. The Spraggs lived
   - ☐ a. in the Rocky Mountains.
   - ☐ b. in the Midwest.
   - ☐ c. along the Atlantic coast.

10. Undine tried to win sympathy from her parents by
    - ☐ a. pretending to be sick.
    - ☐ b. sitting listlessly in the hotel lobby.
    - ☐ c. locking her door and crying all day.

Towards the end of the year 1811, a memorable period for us, the good Gavril Gavrilovitch was living on his domain of Nenaradova. He was celebrated throughout the district for his hospitality and kindheartedness. The neighbors were constantly visiting him: some to eat and drink; some to play at five kopek "Boston" with his wife, Praskovia Petrovna; and some to look at their daughter, Maria Gavrilovna, a pale, slender girl of seventeen. She was considered a wealthy match, and many desired her for themselves or for their sons.

Maria Gavrilovna had been brought up on French novels and consequently was in love. The object of her choice was a poor sub-lieutenant in the army, who was then on leave of absence in his village. It need scarcely be mentioned that the young man returned her passion with equal ardor, and that the parents of his beloved one, observing their mutual inclination, forbade their daughter to think of him, and received him worse than a discharged assessor.

Our lovers corresponded with one another and daily saw each other alone in the little pine wood or near the old chapel. There they exchanged vows of eternal love, lamented their cruel fate, and formed various plans. Corresponding and conversing in this way, they arrived quite naturally at the following conclusion:

If we cannot exist without each other, and the will of hardhearted parents stands in the way of our happiness, why cannot we do without them?

Needless to mention that this happy idea originated in the mind of the young man, and that it was very congenial to the romantic imagination of Maria Gavrilovna.

The winter came and put a stop to their meetings, but their correspondence became all the more active. Vladimir Nikolaievitch in every letter implored her to give herself to him, to get married secretly, to hide for some time, and then to throw themselves at the feet of their parents, who would, without any doubt be touched at last by the heroic constancy and unhappiness of the lovers, and would infallibly say to them: "Children, come to our arms!"

Maria Gavrilovna hesitated for a long time, and several plans for a flight were rejected. At last she consented: on the appointed day she was not to take supper, but was to retire to her room under the pretext of a headache. Her maid was in the plot.

Recalling Facts

1. Gavril Gavrilovitch was noted for his
   - ☐ a. greed.
   - ☐ b. hospitality.
   - ☐ c. temper.

2. Maria was
   - ☐ a. thirty years old.
   - ☐ b. twenty-two years old.
   - ☐ c. seventeen years old.

3. Maria spent much of her time
   - ☐ a. reading French novels.
   - ☐ b. studying Greek classics.
   - ☐ c. writing love poems.

4. Maria fell in love with a
   - ☐ a. sub-lieutenant.
   - ☐ b. sergeant major.
   - ☐ c. lieutenant colonel.

5. Maria and Vladimir plotted to
   - ☐ a. attend a local dance.
   - ☐ b. steal the family jewels.
   - ☐ c. run away and get married.

Understanding the Passage

6. "Boston" appeared to be
   - ☐ a. some kind of game.
   - ☐ b. a nightclub.
   - ☐ c. a person's nickname.

7. Maria's parents thought Vladimir was
   - ☐ a. a fine match for their daughter.
   - ☐ b. beneath Maria's social class.
   - ☐ c. much too old for Maria.

8. Maria's parents
   - ☐ a. didn't want an expensive wedding.
   - ☐ b. wanted to protect her.
   - ☐ c. believed in love at first sight.

9. Maria was in love with
   - ☐ a. the idea of love.
   - ☐ b. Vladimir.
   - ☐ c. both a and b.

10. The two lovers thought that Maria's parents would be impressed
    - ☐ a. if Vladimir was more prominent socially.
    - ☐ b. if Vladimir didn't see Maria for a while.
    - ☐ c. by their undying devotion to each other.

That very singular man, old Dr. Heidegger, once invited four venerable friends to meet him in his study. There were three white-bearded gentlemen, Mr. Medbourne, Colonel Killigrew, and Mr. Gascoigne, and a withered gentlewoman, whose name was the Widow Wycherly. They were all melancholy old creatures, who had been unfortunate in life, and whose greatest misfortune it was that they were not long ago in their graves. Mr. Medbourne, in the vigor of his age, had been a prosperous merchant, but had lost his all by a frantic speculation, and was now little better than a mendicant. Colonel Killigrew had wasted his best years, and his health and substance, in the pursuit of sinful pleasures, which had given birth to a brood of pains, such as the gout, and diverse other torments of soul and body. Mr. Gascoigne was a ruined politician, a man of evil fame, or at least had been so till time had buried him from the knowledge of the present generation, and made him obscure instead of infamous. As for the Widow Wycherly, tradition tells us that she was a great beauty in her day; but, for a long while past, she had lived in deep seclusion, on account of certain scandalous stories which had prejudiced the gentry of the town against her. It is a circumstance worth mentioning that each of these three old gentlemen, Mr. Medbourne, Colonel Killigrew, and Mr. Gascoigne, were early lovers of the Widow Wycherly, and had once been on the point of cutting each other's throats for her sake. And, before proceeding further, I will merely hint that Dr. Heidegger and all his four guests were sometimes thought to be a little beside themselves, as is not unfrequently the case with old people, when worried either by present troubles or woeful recollections.

"My dear old friends," said Dr. Heidegger, motioning them to be seated, "I am desirous of your assistance in one of those little experiments with which I amuse myself here in my study."

If all stories were true, Dr. Heidegger's study must have been a very curious place. It was a dim, old-fashioned chamber, festooned with cob-webs and besprinkled with antique dust. Around the walls stood several oaken bookcases, the lower shelves of which were filled with rows of gigantic folios and black-letter quartos, and the upper with little parchment-covered duodecimos.

Recalling Facts

1. Mr. Medbourne, Colonel Killigrew, and Mr. Gascoigne all had
   - ☐ a. red hair.
   - ☐ b. green slacks.
   - ☐ c. white beards.

2. Mr. Medbourne had once been a
   - ☐ a. lawyer.
   - ☐ b. merchant.
   - ☐ c. banker.

3. Colonel Killigrew suffered from
   - ☐ a. gout.
   - ☐ b. frostbite.
   - ☐ c. malaria.

4. Widow Wycherly was once known for her
   - ☐ a. beauty.
   - ☐ b. wealth.
   - ☐ c. intelligence.

5. All the characters met in Dr. Heidegger's
   - ☐ a. dining room.
   - ☐ b. study.
   - ☐ c. stable.

Understanding the Passage

6. Heidegger's guests were all quite
   - ☐ a. happy.
   - ☐ b. miserable.
   - ☐ c. rich.

7. Mr. Medbourne was not afraid to
   - ☐ a. take wild risks.
   - ☐ b. admit his mistakes.
   - ☐ c. laugh at himself.

8. People of the present generation
   - ☐ a. knew about Mr. Gascoigne's evil ways.
   - ☐ b. were unaware of Mr. Gascoigne.
   - ☐ c. wanted to emulate Mr. Gascoigne.

9. The three men had once been
   - ☐ a. romantic rivals.
   - ☐ b. commercial rivals.
   - ☐ c. political rivals.

10. Dr. Heidegger was about to use his four guests
   - ☐ a. to remodel his home.
   - ☐ b. in some sort of test.
   - ☐ c. to help write his autobiography.

Dear Son,

I have ever had a pleasure in obtaining any little anecdotes of my ancestors. You may remember the enquiries I made among the remains of my relations when you were with me in England and the journey I undertook for that purpose. Imagining it may be equally agreeable to you to know the circumstances of *my* life—many of which you are yet unacquainted with—and expecting a week's interrupted leisure in my present country retirement, I sit down to write them for you. Besides, there are some other inducements that excite me to this undertaking. From the poverty and obscurity in which I was born and in which I passed my earliest years, I have raised myself to a state of affluence and some degree of celebrity in the world. As constant good fortune has accompanied me even to an advanced period of life, my posterity will perhaps be desirous of learning the means, which I employed, and which, thanks to Providence, so well succeeded with me. They may also deem them fit to be imitated, should any of them find themselves in similar circumstances. That good fortune, when I reflected on it, which is frequently the case, has induced me sometimes to say that were it left to my choice, I should have no objection to go over the same life from its beginning to the end, only asking the advantage authors have of correcting in a second edition some faults of the first. So would I also wish to change some incidents of it for others more favorable. Notwithstanding, if this condition were denied, I should still accept the offer. But as this repetition is not to be expected, that which resembles most living one's life over again, seems to be to recall all the circumstances of it; and, to render this remembrance more durable, to record them in writing. In thus employing myself I shall yield to the inclination so natural to old men of talking of themselves and their own actions, and I shall indulge it, without being tiresome to those who, from respect to my age, might conceive themselves obliged to listen to me, since they will be always free to read me or not. And lastly (I may as well confess it, as the denial of it would be believed by nobody) I shall perhaps not a little gratify my own vanity.

Recalling Facts

1. At this time, the narrator was
   - □ a. correcting a book's second edition.
   - □ b. enjoying a country retirement.
   - □ c. an elected official.

2. The narrator was born into
   - □ a. a wealthy family.
   - □ b. a poor, but noble, family.
   - □ c. poverty.

3. The narrator believed his good fortune was due in part to
   - □ a. Providence.
   - □ b. his father-in-law.
   - □ c. his relations in England.

4. The narrator wanted a more permanent record of his
   - □ a. life.
   - □ b. son's business.
   - □ c. both a and b.

5. The narrator feels that old men are naturally inclined to
   - □ a. forget their mistakes.
   - □ b. write an autobiography.
   - □ c. talk about themselves.

Understanding the Passage

6. The purpose of the narrator's trip to England was to
   - □ a. write his autobiography.
   - □ b. explore his family history.
   - □ c. visit high public officials.

7. The narrator feels that his son
   - □ a. lacks education.
   - □ b. shares his values.
   - □ c. is in difficult trouble.

8. The narrator would most like to
   - □ a. live forever.
   - □ b. relive his life exactly.
   - □ c. relive his life with some changes.

9. The narrator's way of reliving his life was to
   - □ a. rectify all earlier mistakes.
   - □ b. forget about it.
   - □ c. write about it.

10. The narrator apparently had his fair share to
    - □ a. guilt.
    - □ b. regrets.
    - □ c. conceit.

Wilfred Thorne, Esq., of Ullathorne, was the squire of St. Ewold's; or rather the squire of Ullathorne; for the domain of the modern landlord was of wider notoriety than the fame of the ancient saint. He was a fair specimen of what that race has come to, which a century ago was, as we are told, fairly represented by Squire Western. If that representation be a true one, few classes of men can have made faster strides in improvement. Mr. Thorne, however, was a man possessed of quite a sufficient number of foibles to lay him open to ridicule. He was still a bachelor, being about fifty, and was not a little proud of his person. When living at home at Ullathorne there was not much room for such pride, and there therefore he always looked like a gentleman, and like that which he certainly was, the first man in his parish. But during the month or six weeks which he annually spent in London, he tried so hard to look like a great man there also, which he certainly was not, that he was put down as a fool by many. He was a man of considerable literary attainment on certain subjects; his favorite authors were Montaigne and Burton, and he knew more perhaps than any other man in his own county, and the one next to it, of the English essayists of the two last centuries. He possessed complete sets of the "Idler," the "Spectator," the "Tatler," the "Guardian," and the "Rambler"; and would discourse by hours together on the superiority of such publications to anything which has since been produced in our Edinburghs and Quarter-lies. He was a great proficient in all questions of genealogy, and knew enough of almost every gentleman's family in England to say of what blood and lineage were descended all those who had any claim to be considered as possessors of any such luxuries. For blood and lineage he himself had a most profound respect. He counted back his own ancestors to some period long antecedent to the Conquest; and could tell you, if you would listen to him, how it had come to pass that they, like Cedric the Saxon, had been permitted to hold their own among the Norman barons. It was not, according to his showing, on account of any weak complaisance on the part of his family towards their Norman neighbors.

Recalling Facts

1. Wilfred Thorne was the squire of
   - ☐ a. St. Ewold's.
   - ☐ b. Ullathorne.
   - ☐ c. both a and b.

2. Thorne was
   - ☐ a. still a bachelor.
   - ☐ b. about thirty-five years old.
   - ☐ c. both a and b.

3. Every year Thorne spent about a month in
   - ☐ a. Scotland.
   - ☐ b. Dublin.
   - ☐ c. London.

4. Burton and Montaigne were famous
   - ☐ a. artists.
   - ☐ b. writers.
   - ☐ c. scientists.

5. Thorne had a special interest in
   - ☐ a. geology.
   - ☐ b. geography.
   - ☐ c. genealogy.

Understanding the Passage

6. The people of Ullathorne were
   - ☐ a. better educated than most people in London.
   - ☐ b. less sophisticated than most people in London.
   - ☐ c. richer than most people in London.

7. Thorne was often
   - ☐ a. laughed at by people in London.
   - ☐ b. called to assist the archbishop.
   - ☐ c. rejected by publishers.

8. Thorne had an overblown sense of
   - ☐ a. fear.
   - ☐ b. tragedy.
   - ☐ c. self-worth.

9. Literature
   - ☐ a. bored Thorne.
   - ☐ b. was one of Thorne's great passions.
   - ☐ c. wasn't studied by men of Thorne's class.

10. Thorne wanted to show that his ancestors were not
    - ☐ a. cowards.
    - ☐ b. peasants.
    - ☐ c. uneducated.

We all were glad to see him; on his return he had found us all his friends. Nobody had spoken to him about his abrupt departure from New York; nobody had mentioned Westover; nothing connected with that episode was even hinted at by any of us, I believe, during his short sojourn among us. It was he himself who spoke of it first.

Of course during his absence we had followed his career; many among us had read and tried to understand what he had written in his three world-famous volumes, "Occult Philosophy," "The Weight of Human Souls," and "The Interstellar Laws of Psychic Phenomena."

It seemed, at times, here to us in America, that it was impossible that the man we had known so well could have become the great Psychic Scientist who had written these three astounding works—who now occupied the Chair of Psychical Philosophy in the great University of Trebizond—the man who was the confidential adviser of the Shah of Persia, the mentor of the Ameer of Afghanistan, the inspirer of the greatest diplomat of all the East—the late Akhound of Swat.

As he sat there in his immaculate evening dress, bronzed, youthful looking, presiding so quietly at the little dinner which he had given to us as a half-formal, half-intimate leave-taking before he sailed, it seemed to us incredible that this man, now on his return journey to Trebizond via Lhassa, could be the beloved and dreaded arbiter of Asiatic politics—the one white man in all the Orient who had ever been wholly respected, and absolutely feared by the temporal and spiritual heads of nations, religions, clans, and sects.

That, of course, he was what is popularly known as an adept, we supposed. What his wisdom, his insight, his amazing knowledge of the occult might include, we preferred, rather uncomfortably, not to conjecture.

There is, naturally, in all of us a childlike desire to hear of marvels; there is also a stronger and more childish desire to see miracles performed.

I am quite sure that we all hoped he might perhaps care to do something for us—merely to convince us. And at first, I know that many among us, seated there in the private room at the Lenox Club, felt a trifle ill at ease and a little in awe of this man with whom we were at such close quarters.

Recalling Facts

1. The famous man wrote books about
   - ☐ a. political intrigue.
   - ☐ b. the occult.
   - ☐ c. the ocean.

2. Trebizond was a
   - ☐ a. country.
   - ☐ b. foreign leader.
   - ☐ c. university.

3. The Akhound of Swat was the
   - ☐ a. Ameer of Afghanistan.
   - ☐ b. Shah of Persia.
   - ☐ c. greatest diplomat of all the East.

4. The famous man would soon be
   - ☐ a. returning to Trebizond.
   - ☐ b. giving a lecture at the Lenox Club.
   - ☐ c. declared the Shah of Persia.

5. The dinner guests most wanted to
   - ☐ a. see miracles performed.
   - ☐ b. hear about miracles.
   - ☐ c. talk about Westover.

Understanding the Passage

6. The episode regarding Westover was
   - ☐ a. soon forgotten.
   - ☐ b. frequently discussed.
   - ☐ c. a rather sensitive topic.

7. The famous man had been away for
   - ☐ a. a few days.
   - ☐ b. several weeks.
   - ☐ c. a long time.

8. The dinner guests
   - ☐ a. were angered at the success of their host.
   - ☐ b. were unfamiliar with their host's accomplishments.
   - ☐ c. had trouble understanding their host's success.

9. Among Asians, the famous man had
   - ☐ a. some respect.
   - ☐ b. incredible power.
   - ☐ c. lost his prestige.

10. Before becoming famous the man had been
    - ☐ a. a failure at most things.
    - ☐ b. close friends with the dinner guests.
    - ☐ c. an import-export dealer.

The outward relations between James and his son were marked by a lack of sentiment, but for all that the two were by no means unattached. Perhaps they regarded one another as an investment; certainly they were solicitous of each other's welfare, glad of each other's company. They had never exchanged two words upon the more intimate problems of life, or revealed in each other's presence the existence of any deep feeling.

Something beyond the power of word analysis bound them together, something hidden deep in the fiber of nations and families—for blood, they say, is thicker than water—and neither of them was a cold-blooded man. Indeed, in James love of his children was now the prime motive of his existence. To have creatures who were parts of himself, to whom he might transmit the money he saved, was at the root of his saving; and, at seventy-five, what was left that could give him pleasure, but—saving? The kernel of life was in this saving for his children.

Than James Forsyte, notwithstanding all his "Jonah-isms," there was no saner man in all this London, of which he owned so much, and loved with such a dumb love, as the center of his opportunities. He had the marvelous instinctive sanity of the middle class. In him—more than in Jolyon, with his masterful will and his moments of tenderness and philosophy—more than in Swithin, the martyr to crankiness—Nicholas, the sufferer from ability—and Roger, the victim of enterprise—beat the true pulse of compromise; of all the brothers he was least remarkable in mind and person, and for that reason more likely to live forever.

To James, more than to any of the others, was "the family" significant and dear. There had always been something primitive and cozy in his attitude towards life; he loved the family hearth, he loved gossip, and he loved grumbling. All his decisions were formed of a cream which he skimmed off the family mind; and, through that family, off the minds of thousands of other families of similar fiber. Year after year, week after week, he went to Timothy's, and in his brother's front drawing room—his legs twisted, his long white whiskers framing his clean-shaven mouth—would sit watching the family pot simmer, the cream rising to the top; and he would go away sheltered, refreshed, comforted, with an indefinable sense of comfort.

Recalling Facts

1. Neither James nor his son
   - ☐ a. had money.
   - ☐ b. was cold-blooded.
   - ☐ c. loved children.

2. James was
   - ☐ a. fairly young.
   - ☐ b. middle-aged.
   - ☐ c. an old man.

3. James got pleasure by
   - ☐ a. spending time in London.
   - ☐ b. saving money.
   - ☐ c. talking with his son.

4. The person known for his strong will was
   - ☐ a. Swithin.
   - ☐ b. Nicholas.
   - ☐ c. Jolyon.

5. Swithin, Jolyon, Nicholas, and Roger were James's
   - ☐ a. business partners.
   - ☐ b. sons.
   - ☐ c. brothers.

Understanding the Passage

6. James and his son were
   - ☐ a. not openly affectionate toward each other.
   - ☐ b. not on speaking terms.
   - ☐ c. extremely close in all ways.

7. The relationship between James and his son was
   - ☐ a. hard to explain.
   - ☐ b. a source of great conflict.
   - ☐ c. like that of all fathers and sons.

8. According to the narrator, a person without any remarkable traits was likely to
   - ☐ a. have many friends.
   - ☐ b. have a large family.
   - ☐ c. live to a ripe old age.

9. James was powerfully influenced by
   - ☐ a. his compulsive impulses.
   - ☐ b. family considerations.
   - ☐ c. the business success of his friends.

10. James spent a lot of his time
   - ☐ a. visiting relatives.
   - ☐ b. working at the bank.
   - ☐ c. tracing his family roots.

As Mr. John Oakhurst, gambler, stepped into the main street of Poker Flat on the morning of the 23rd of November, 1850, he was conscious of a change in its moral atmosphere since the preceding night. Two or three men, conversing earnestly together, ceased as he approached, and exchanged significant glances. There was a Sabbath lull in the air, which, in a settlement unused to Sabbath influences, looked ominous.

Mr. Oakhurst's calm, handsome face betrayed small concern in these indications. Whether he was conscious of any predisposing cause was another question. "I reckon they're after somebody," he reflected; "likely it's me." He returned to his pocket the handkerchief with which he had been wiping away the red dust of Poker Flat from his neat boots, and quietly discharged his mind of any further conjecture.

In point of fact, Poker Flat was "after somebody." It had lately suffered the loss of several thousand dollars, two valuable horses, and a prominent citizen. It was experiencing a spasm of virtuous reaction, quite as lawless and ungovernable as any of the acts that had provoked it. A secret committee had determined to rid the town of all improper persons. This was done permanently in regard to the two men who were then hanging from the boughs of a sycamore, and temporarily in the banishment of certain other objectionable characters. I regret to say that some of these were ladies. It is but due to the sex, however, to state that their impropriety was professional, and it was only in such easily established standards of evil that Poker Flat ventured to sit in judgment.

Mr. Oakhurst was right in supposing that he was included in this category. A few of the committee had urged hanging him as a possible example and a sure method of reimbursing themselves from his pockets of the sums he had won from them. "It's agin' justice," said Jim Wheeler, "to let this here young man from Roaring Camp—an entire stranger—carry away our money." But a crude sentiment of equity residing in the breasts of those who had been fortunate enough to win from Mr. Oakhurst overruled this narrower local prejudice.

Mr. Oakhurst received his sentence with philosophic calmness, none the less coolly that he was aware of the hesitation of his judges. He was too much of a gambler not to accept fate. With him life was at best an uncertain game.

Recalling Facts

1. Mr. Oakhurst earned his living as a
   - ☐ a. preacher.
   - ☐ b. gambler.
   - ☐ c. lawman.

2. Poker Flat had recently lost
   - ☐ a. two horses.
   - ☐ b. several rooming houses.
   - ☐ c. both a and b.

3. A secret committee had already
   - ☐ a. hanged two men.
   - ☐ b. hired a professional gunfighter.
   - ☐ c. fired the sheriff.

4. Mr. Oakhurst was from
   - ☐ a. Poker Flat.
   - ☐ b. Roaring Camp.
   - ☐ c. Wheeler.

5. Mr. Oakhurst received his sentence with
   - ☐ a. great alarm.
   - ☐ b. fierce resistance.
   - ☐ c. philosophic calmness.

Understanding the Passage

6. The men on the street viewed Mr. Oakhurst with
   - ☐ a. suspicion.
   - ☐ b. fear.
   - ☐ c. respect.

7. Mr. Oakhurst's outlook on life was one of
   - ☐ a. deeply felt hostility.
   - ☐ b. strong religious conviction.
   - ☐ c. casual acceptance.

8. Poker Flat appeared to be a town without
   - ☐ a. nightclubs and barrooms.
   - ☐ b. organized law enforcement.
   - ☐ c. a concerned group of citizens.

9. The ladies who were being run out of town were probably
   - ☐ a. gamblers.
   - ☐ b. saloon girls.
   - ☐ c. waitresses.

10. Mr. Oakhurst was saved from hanging by
    - ☐ a. the sheriff.
    - ☐ b. those who had won money from him.
    - ☐ c. the town's ladies.

During all these desperate years in Brooklyn, when George Webber lived and worked alone, he had only one real friend, and this was his editor, Foxhall Edwards. They spent many hours together, wonderful hours of endless talk, so free and full that it combed the universe and bound the two of them together in bonds of closest friendship. It was a friendship founded on many common tastes and interests, on mutual liking and admiration of each for what the other was, and on an attitude of respect which allowed unhampered expression of opinion even on those rare subjects which aroused differences of views and of belief. It was, therefore, the kind of friendship that can exist only between two men. It had in it no element of that possessiveness which always threatens a woman's relations with a man, no element of that physical and emotional involvement which, while it serves nature's end of bringing a man and woman together, also tends to thwart their own dearest wish to remain so by throwing over their companionship a constricting cloak of duty and obligation, of right and vested interest.

The older man was not merely friend but father to the younger. Webber, the hot-blooded Southerner, with his large capacity for sentiment and affection, had lost his own father many years before and now had found a substitute in Edwards. And Edwards, the reserved New Englander, with his deep sense of family and inheritance, had always wanted a son but had had five daughters, and as time went on he made of George a kind of foster son. Thus each, without quite knowing that he did it, performed an act of spiritual adoption.

So it was to Foxhall Edwards that George now turned whenever his loneliness became unbearable. When his inner turmoil, confusion, and self-doubts overwhelmed him, as they often did, and his life went dead and stale and empty till it sometimes seemed that all the barren desolation of the Brooklyn streets had soaked into his very blood and marrow—then he would seek out Edwards. And he never went to him in vain. Edwards, busy though he always was, would drop whatever he was doing and would take George out to lunch or dinner, and in his quiet, casual, oblique, and understanding way would talk to him and draw him out until he found out what it was that troubled him.

Recalling Facts

1. Foxhall Edwards was George's
   - ☐ a. landlord.
   - ☐ b. editor.
   - ☐ c. brother.

2. Edward and George talked
   - ☐ a. mainly about business affairs.
   - ☐ b. only when their daily work was complete.
   - ☐ c. about many different things.

3. The element that threatens relations between men and women is
   - ☐ a. free expression of opinion.
   - ☐ b. overwhelming friendship.
   - ☐ c. possessiveness.

4. Edwards was from
   - ☐ a. New England.
   - ☐ b. the South.
   - ☐ c. England.

5. Edwards had
   - ☐ a. five daughters.
   - ☐ b. five sons.
   - ☐ c. no family.

Understanding the Passage

6. Edwards and George
   - ☐ a. never disagreed about anything.
   - ☐ b. disagreed only about a few things.
   - ☐ c. never established a close friendship.

7. The relationship between a married man and woman tends to be
   - ☐ a. constrained by increased responsibilities.
   - ☐ b. not nearly as restrictive as it should be.
   - ☐ c. strengthened by the passage of years.

8. George helped Edwards
   - ☐ a. out of financial trouble.
   - ☐ b. by serving as his "adopted" son.
   - ☐ c. rewrite much of his work.

9. George needed Edwards most when he was
   - ☐ a. miserable.
   - ☐ b. happy and working.
   - ☐ c. returning from Brooklyn.

10. The narrator implies that New Englanders
    - ☐ a. tend not to be very demonstrative.
    - ☐ b. do not like Southerners.
    - ☐ c. make poor businessmen.

I went blueberrying with Mrs. Alderling in the morning, after she finished putting her breakfast dishes away, in order that we might have something for dessert at our midday dinner; and I went fishing off the old stone crib with Mr. Alderling in the afternoon, so that we might have cunners for supper. The farmerfolks and fisherfolks seemed to know them and to be on tolerant terms with them, though it was plain that they still considered them probational in their fellow citizenship. I do not think they were liked the less because they did not assume to be of the local sort, but let their difference stand, if it would. There was nothing countrified in her dress, which was frankly conventional; the short walking skirt had as sharp a slant in front as her dinner gown would have had, and he wore his knickerbockers—it was then the now-faded hour of knickerbockers—with an air of going out golfing in the suburbs. She had stayed on with him through the first winter in the cottage they had taken for the summer, because she wished to be with him, rather than because she wished to be there, and he had stayed because he had not found just the moment to break away, though afterwards he pretended a reason for staying. They had no more voluntarily cultivated the natural than the supernatural; he kindled the fire for her, and she made the coffee for him, not because they preferred, but because they must; and they had arrived at their common ground in the occult by virtue of being alone together, and not by seeking the solitude for the experiment which the solitude promoted. Mrs. Alderling did not talk less nor he more when either was alone with me than when we were all together; perhaps he was more silent and she not quite so much; she was making up for him in his absence as he was for her in her presence. But they were always hospitable and attentive hosts, and though under the peculiar circumstances of Mrs. Alderling's having to do the housework herself I necessarily had to do a good many things for myself, there were certain little graces which were never wanting from her hands: my curtains were always carefully drawn, and my coverlet triangularly opened, so that I did not have to pull it down myself.

Recalling Facts

1. In the morning, the narrator and Mrs. Alderling
   - ☐ a. shopped together.
   - ☐ b. picked blueberries.
   - ☐ c. went fishing.

2. In his knickerbockers, Mr. Alderling looked like he was
   - ☐ a. going fishing.
   - ☐ b. heading for the golf course.
   - ☐ c. a country gardener.

3. The housework was done by
   - ☐ a. a maid.
   - ☐ b. Mrs. Alderling.
   - ☐ c. the Alderlings' daughter.

4. The narrator felt the Alderlings were
   - ☐ a. quite pretentious.
   - ☐ b. attentive hosts.
   - ☐ c. ostensibly overeducated.

5. The narrator never had to
   - ☐ a. pull down the coverlet on his bed.
   - ☐ b. seek a partner for fishing and golfing.
   - ☐ c. carry on a conversation with Mr. Alderling.

Understanding the Passage

6. Mr. and Mrs. Alderling had not
   - ☐ a. grown up in this area.
   - ☐ b. spent any winters in this area.
   - ☐ c. been married for long.

7. Mrs. Alderling did not want to
   - ☐ a. wear walking skirts.
   - ☐ b. spend winters away from her husband.
   - ☐ c. talk to the narrator about the past.

8. The narrator
   - ☐ a. helped the Alderlings with daily chores.
   - ☐ b. did not like helping Mr. Alderling.
   - ☐ c. spent the entire day fishing.

9. The Alderlings had not planned on
   - ☐ a. becoming involved in the occult.
   - ☐ b. marrying each other.
   - ☐ c. hosting the narrator.

10. The Alderlings apparently did not
    - ☐ a. believe in the supernatural.
    - ☐ b. enjoy the respect of their neighbors.
    - ☐ c. alter their life much to accommodate the narrator.

It was about the beginning of September 1664, that I, among the rest of my neighbors, heard, in ordinary discourse, that the plague was returned again in Holland; for it had been very violent there, and particularly at Amsterdam and Rotterdam, in the year 1663, whither, they say, it was brought, some said from Italy, others from Levant; others said it was brought from Candia; others from Cyprus. It mattered not from whence it came; but all agreed it was come into Holland again.

We had no such thing as printed newspapers in those days to spread rumors and reports of things, and to improve them by the invention of men. But such things as those were gathered from the letters of merchants and others who corresponded abroad, and from them was handed about by word of mouth only; so that things did not spread instantly over the whole nation. But it seems that the government had a true account of it, and several councils were held about ways to prevent its coming over; but all was kept very private. Hence it was that this rumor died off again, and people began to forget it, as a thing we were very little concerned in, and that we hoped was not true, till the latter end of November or the beginning of December 1664, when two men, said to be Frenchmen, died of the plague in Long Acre, or rather at the upper end of Drury Lane. The family they were in endeavored to conceal it as much as possible, but as it had gotten some vent in the discourse of the neighborhood, the Secretaries of State got knowledge of it, and concerning themselves to inquire about it, in order to be certain of the truth, two physicians and a surgeon were ordered to go to the house and make inspection. This they did; and finding evident tokens of the sickness upon both the bodies that were dead, they gave their opinions publicly that they died of the plague. Whereupon it was given in to the parish clerk, and he also returned them to the hall; and it was printed in the weekly bill of mortality in the usual manner. The people showed a great concern at this, and began to be alarmed all over the town, because in the last week in December 1664 another man died.

Recalling Facts

1. In 1664, the narrator heard that the plague had returned to
   ☐ a. Cyprus.
   ☐ b. Italy.
   ☐ c. Holland.

2. The source of this plague was
   ☐ a. the Levant.
   ☐ b. Candia.
   ☐ c. uncertain.

3. The news of the outbreak of the plague
   ☐ a. spread slowly.
   ☐ b. was carried in all the newspapers.
   ☐ c. was announced by church leaders.

4. The two men who died of the plague around the first of December 1664 were
   ☐ a. Englishmen.
   ☐ b. Frenchmen.
   ☐ c. Italians.

5. The cause of the two deaths was confirmed by
   ☐ a. the parish clerk.
   ☐ b. the narrator.
   ☐ c. medical experts.

Understanding the Passage

6. At this time, the biggest issue was
   ☐ a. where the plague came from.
   ☐ b. whether the plague really had returned.
   ☐ c. how the plague was being spread.

7. The truth about the two dead men from Drury Lane
   ☐ a. was nearly impossible to keep secret.
   ☐ b. was disregarded by the Secretaries of State.
   ☐ c. set off riots in several major cities.

8. The people had
   ☐ a. no previous experience with the plague.
   ☐ b. developed measures to prevent the plague.
   ☐ c. suffered from the plague before.

9. Doctors could prove that the plague was the cause of a man's death by
   ☐ a. examining the dead body.
   ☐ b. calling in the mortician.
   ☐ c. questioning his family.

10. When people learned that the plague had returned, they
    ☐ a. left town hurriedly.
    ☐ b. denounced the Secretaries of State.
    ☐ c. became quite worried.

Having parted from my friend, I determined to visit some remote location in Scotland and finish my work in solitude. With this resolution I traversed the northern highlands, and settled on one of the remotest of the Orkneys as the scene of my labors. It was a place fitted for my work, being hardly more than a rock, whose high sides were continually beaten upon by the waves, and whose soil was barren, scarcely affording pasture for a few miserable cows, and oatmeal for its inhabitants, which consisted of five persons, whose gaunt and scraggy limbs gave tokens of their miserable diets. Vegetables and bread, when they indulged in such luxuries, and even fresh water, was to be procured from the mainland, which was approximately five miles distant.

On the whole island there were but three miserable huts, and one of these was vacant when I arrived, so I rented it. It contained only two rooms, and these exhibited all the squalidness of the most miserable penury. The thatch had fallen in, the walls were unplastered, and the door was off its hinges. I ordered it to be repaired, purchased some furniture, and took possession; an incident which would, undoubtedly, have occasioned some surprise, had not all the senses of the cottagers been benumbed by want and squalid poverty. As it was, I lived ungazed at and unmolested, hardly thanked for the pittance of food and clothing which I gave; so much does suffering blunt even the coarsest sensations of men.

In this retreat I devoted mornings to labor; but in the evenings, when the weather permitted, I walked on the stony beach, listening to the waves as they roared and dashed at my feet. It was a monotonous yet ever-changing scene. I thought of Switzerland; it was distinctly different from this desolate and appalling landscape. Its hills are covered with vines, and its cottages are scattered thickly in the plains; its fair lakes reflect a blue and gentle sky, and, when troubled by the winds, their tumult is but as the play of a lively infant, when compared to the roarings of the giant ocean.

In this manner I distributed my occupations when I first arrived; but, as I proceeded in my labor, it became every day more horrible and irksome to me, so that sometimes I could not prevail on myself to enter my laboratory for several days.

Recalling Facts

1. The narrator went to a remote spot in Scotland to
   - ☐ a. reflect on his life.
   - ☐ b. work undisturbed.
   - ☐ c. help the natives.

2. The narrator picked a spot inhabited only by a few
   - ☐ a. people and cows.
   - ☐ b. cows and goats.
   - ☐ c. wolves and people.

3. On the entire island there were only
   - ☐ a. two huts.
   - ☐ b. three huts.
   - ☐ c. ten huts.

4. In the evening, the narrator often
   - ☐ a. hiked up into the mountains.
   - ☐ b. walked along the seashore.
   - ☐ c. relaxed with the natives.

5. The narrator devoted his mornings to
   - ☐ a. exercise.
   - ☐ b. work.
   - ☐ c. reading.

Understanding the Passage

6. The narrator felt the natives were living
   - ☐ a. wretched lives.
   - ☐ b. ordinary lives.
   - ☐ c. idyllic lives.

7. The islanders apparently didn't have any excess
   - ☐ a. food.
   - ☐ b. time.
   - ☐ c. space.

8. Among the natives, the narrator's appearance caused
   - ☐ a. great excitement.
   - ☐ b. hardly any interest.
   - ☐ c. considerable conversation.

9. The narrator seemed a bit homesick for
   - ☐ a. the Orkneys.
   - ☐ b. Switzerland.
   - ☐ c. England.

10. As time went by, the narrator had less and less
    - ☐ a. opportunity to be alone.
    - ☐ b. desire to leave the island.
    - ☐ c. enthusiasm for his work.

The shallow sea that foams and murmurs on the shores of the thousand islands, big and little, which make up the Malay Archipelago has been for centuries the scene of adventurous undertakings. The vices and the qualities of four nations have been displayed in the conquest of that region that even to this day has not been robbed of all the mystery and romance of its past—and the race of men who had fought against the Portuguese, the Spaniards, the Dutch and the English, has not been changed by the unavoidable defeat. They have kept to this day their love of liberty, their fanatical devotion to their chiefs, their blind fidelity in friendship and hate—all their lawful and unlawful instincts. Their country of land and water—for the sea was as much their country as the earth of their islands—has fallen a prey to the western race—the reward of superior strength if not of superior value. Tomorrow the advancing civilization shall obliterate the marks of a long struggle in the accomplishment of its inevitable victory.

The adventurers who began that struggle have left no descendants. The ideas of the world changed too quick for that. But even far into the present century they have had successors. Almost in our own day we have seen one of them—a true adventurer in his devotion to his impulse—a man of high mind and of pure heart, lay the foundation of a flourishing state on the ideas of pity and justice. He recognized chivalrously the claims of the conquered; he was a disinterested adventurer, and the reward of his noble instincts is in the veneration with which a strange and faithful race cherish his memory.

Misunderstood and traduced in life, the glory of his achievement has vindicated the purity of his motives: he belongs to history. But there were others—obscure adventurers who had not his advantages of birth, position and intelligence; who had only his sympathy with the people of forests and sea he understood and loved so well. They were lost in the common crowd of seamen-traders of the Archipelago, and if they emerged from their obscurity it was only to be condemned as law breakers. Their lives were thrown away for a cause that had no right to exist in the face of an irresistible and orderly progress—their thoughtless lives guided by a simple feeling.

Recalling Facts

1. Among the nations that tried to conquer the Malay Archipelago was
   - ☐ a. France.
   - ☐ b. Portugal.
   - ☐ c. Sweden.

2. According to the narrator, the victory of western powers was
   - ☐ a. avoidable.
   - ☐ b. a good thing.
   - ☐ c. inevitable.

3. The narrator believed the ideas of the world change
   - ☐ a. much too slowly.
   - ☐ b. at regular intervals.
   - ☐ c. quickly.

4. The last true adventurer was now
   - ☐ a. a part of history.
   - ☐ b. hated by the natives.
   - ☐ c. forgotten by nearly everyone.

5. If obscure adventurers were thought of at all, it was because they
   - ☐ a. broke the law.
   - ☐ b. wrote a book.
   - ☐ c. sailed unusual distances.

Understanding the Passage

6. The western nations
   - ☐ a. destroyed the Malay Archipelago.
   - ☐ b. irreversibly changed the Malay Archipelago.
   - ☐ c. saved the culture of the Malay Archipelago.

7. The natives who fought against the westerners
   - ☐ a. were foolish to try.
   - ☐ b. needed the advantages of civilization.
   - ☐ c. held on to their basic principles.

8. The natives
   - ☐ a. respected one western adventurer.
   - ☐ b. hated all westerners.
   - ☐ c. lacked a sense of fidelity in friendship.

9. The adventurer who "belongs to history" was
   - ☐ a. better loved after his death.
   - ☐ b. criticized by other famous western adventurers.
   - ☐ c. unable to follow through on his ideas.

10. Most obscure adventurers
    - ☐ a. were nothing more than petty criminals.
    - ☐ b. favored the march of progress.
    - ☐ c. loved and supported the native people.

from **The Name-Day** *by H. H. Munro*

Adventures, according to the proverb, are to the adventurous. John James Abbleway had been endowed by Nature with the sort of disposition that instinctively avoids intrigues, slum crusades, the tracking of wounded wild beasts, and the moving of hostile amendments at political meetings. If a mad dog or a Mad Mullah had come his way he would have surrendered the way without hesitation. At school he had unwillingly acquired a thorough knowledge of the German tongue out of deference to the plainly expressed wishes of a foreign languages master, who, though he taught modern subjects, employed old-fashioned methods in driving his lessons home. It was this enforced familiarity with an important commercial language which thrust Abbleway in later years into strange lands where adventures were less easy to guard against than in the ordered atmosphere of an English country town. The firm that he worked for saw fit to send him one day on a prosaic business errand to the far city of Vienna, and, having sent him there, continued to keep him there, still engaged in humdrum affairs of commerce, but with the possibilities of romance and adventure, or even misadventure, jostling at his elbow. After two and a half years of exile, however, John James Abbleway had embarked on only one hazardous undertaking, and that was of a nature which would assuredly have overtaken him sooner or later if he had been leading a sheltered, stay-at-home existence at Dorking or Huntingdon. He fell placidly in love with a placidly lovable English girl, the sister of one of his commercial colleagues, who was improving her mind by a short trip to foreign parts, and in due course he was formally accepted as the young man she was engaged to. The further step by which she was to become Mrs. John Abbleway was to take place twelve months hence in a town in the English midlands, by which time the firm that employed John James would have no further need for his presence in the Austrian capital.

It was early in April, two months after the installation of Abbleway as the young man Miss Penning was engaged to, when he received a letter from her, written from Venice. She was still traveling under the wing of her brother. She had conceived the idea that it would be rather jolly if John could run down to the Adriatic coast to meet them.

Recalling Facts

1. At school James Abbleway learned to speak fluent
   - ☐ a. French.
   - ☐ b. Spanish.
   - ☐ c. German.

2. The foreign language master
   - ☐ a. was an incompetent instructor.
   - ☐ b. used the latest teaching methods.
   - ☐ c. stuck to old-fashioned techniques.

3. One day his firm sent James to
   - ☐ a. Huntingdon.
   - ☐ b. London.
   - ☐ c. Vienna.

4. James fell in love with
   - ☐ a. an English girl.
   - ☐ b. a German woman.
   - ☐ c. an Austrian widow.

5. Miss Penning was traveling with her
   - ☐ a. girlfriend.
   - ☐ b. brother.
   - ☐ c. mother.

Understanding the Passage

6. James could best be described as
   - ☐ a. daring and brave.
   - ☐ b. outgoing and aggressive.
   - ☐ c. cautious and timid.

7. Vienna at this time was
   - ☐ a. very similar to Dorking.
   - ☐ b. an adventurous place.
   - ☐ c. little more than a sleepy town.

8. James apparently was
   - ☐ a. open to new experiences.
   - ☐ b. interested in doing only safe things.
   - ☐ c. aggressively pursuing risky business decisions.

9. After two and a half years of living overseas, James
   - ☐ a. discovered many new things about himself.
   - ☐ b. learned to take chances.
   - ☐ c. had not changed his basic nature.

10. Miss Penning seemed to
    - ☐ a. enjoy traveling.
    - ☐ b. distrust John.
    - ☐ c. be much older than John.

The discipline of the family, in those days, was of a far more rigid kind than now. The frown, the harsh rebuke, the frequent application of the rod, enjoined by Scriptural authority, were used, not merely in the way of punishment for actual offenses, but as a wholesome regimen for the growth and promotion of all childish virtues. Hester Prynne, nevertheless, the lonely mother of this one child, ran little risk of erring on the side of undue severity. Mindful of her own errors and misfortunes, she early sought to impose a tender, but strict control over the infant immortality that was committed to her charge. But the task was beyond her skill. After testing both smiles and frowns, and proving that neither mode of treatment possessed any calculable influence, Hester was ultimately compelled to stand aside, and permit the child to be swayed by her own impulses. Physical compulsion or restraint was effectual, of course, while it lasted. As to any other kind of discipline, whether addressed to her mind or heart, little Pearl might or might not be within its reach, in accordance with the caprice that ruled the moment. Her mother, while Pearl was yet an infant, grew acquainted with a certain peculiar look, that warned her when it would be labor thrown away to insist, persuade, or plead. It was a look so intelligent, yet inexplicable, so perverse, sometimes so malicious, but generally accompanied by a wild flow of spirits, that Hester could not help questioning, at such moments, whether Pearl was a human child. She seemed rather an airy sprite, which, after playing its fantastic sports for a little while upon the cottage floor, would flit away with a mocking smile. Whenever that look appeared in her wild, bright, deeply black eyes, it invested her with a strange remoteness and intangibility; it was as if she were hovering in the air and might vanish, like a glimmering light, that comes we know not whence, and goes we know not whither. Beholding it, Hester was constrained to rush towards the child—to pursue the little elf in the flight which she invariably began, to snatch her to her bosom, with a close pressure and earnest kisses, not so much from overflowing love, as to assure herself that Pearl was flesh and blood, and not utterly delusive. But Pearl's laugh, when caught, made her mother more doubtful than before.

Recalling Facts

1. Hester Prynne had
   - ☐ a. one child.
   - ☐ b. two children.
   - ☐ c. three children.

2. The infant's name was
   - ☐ a. Hester.
   - ☐ b. Rodney.
   - ☐ c. Pearl.

3. Hester wondered whether her child was
   - ☐ a. intelligent.
   - ☐ b. honest.
   - ☐ c. human.

4. Pearl's eyes were
   - ☐ a. blue.
   - ☐ b. brown.
   - ☐ c. black.

5. After catching Pearl, Hester gave her
   - ☐ a. a severe beating.
   - ☐ b. a stern lecture.
   - ☐ c. earnest kisses.

Understanding the Passage

6. Using a rod to discipline a child was approved in
   - ☐ a. the Bible.
   - ☐ b. the Constitution.
   - ☐ c. both a and b.

7. People believed that physical punishment was good for
   - ☐ a. the soul.
   - ☐ b. the body.
   - ☐ c. only some children.

8. Hester Prynne was not a
   - ☐ a. good mother.
   - ☐ b. harsh disciplinarian.
   - ☐ c. young woman.

9. Pearl can best be described as
   - ☐ a. passive.
   - ☐ b. headstrong.
   - ☐ c. pensive.

10. Hester's efforts to discipline her child
    - ☐ a. made her question her own ability.
    - ☐ b. gave her a sense of achievement.
    - ☐ c. were approved of by her family.

I shall not easily forget the first time I ever saw Abraham Lincoln. It must have been about the 18th or 19th of February, 1861. It was rather a pleasant afternoon, in New York City, as he arrived there from the West, to remain a few hours, and then pass on to Washington, to prepare for his inauguration. I saw him on Broadway, near the site of the present post office. He came down, I think from Canal street, to stop at the Astor House. The broad spaces, sidewalks, and streets in the neighborhood were crowded with solid masses of people, many thousands. The omnibuses and other vehicles had all been turned off, leaving an unusual hush in that busy part of the city. Presently two or three shabby hack carriages made their way with some difficulty through the crowd, and drew up at the Astor House entrance. A tall figure stepped out of the center of these carriages, paused leisurely on the sidewalk, looked up at the granite walls and looming architecture of the grand old hotel—then, after a relieving stretch of arms and legs, turned round for over a minute to slowly and good-humoredly scan the appearance of the vast and silent crowds. There were no speeches—no compliments—no welcome—as far as I could hear, not a word said. Still much anxiety was concealed in that quiet. Cautious persons had feared some marked insult or indignity to the President-elect—for he possessed no personal popularity at all in New York City, and very little political. But it was evidently tacitly agreed that if the few political supporters of Mr. Lincoln present would entirely abstain from any demonstration on their side, the immense majority, who were anything but supporters, would abstain on their side also. The result was a sulky, unbroken silence, such as certainly never before characterized so great a New York crowd.

From the top of an omnibus, I had, I say, a capital view of it all, and especially of Mr. Lincoln, his look and gait—his perfect composure and coolness—his unusual and uncouth height, his dress of complete black, stovepipe hat pushed back on the head, dark brown complexion, seamed and wrinkled yet canny-looking face, black, bushy head of hair, disproportionately long neck, and his hand held behind as he stood observing the people. He looked with curiosity upon that immense sea of faces.

Recalling Facts

1. The narrator first saw Lincoln in
   □ a. New York City.
   □ b. April of 1865.
   □ c. both a and b.

2. When Lincoln arrived at the Astor House, he
   □ a. gave a short speech.
   □ b. stretched his arms and legs.
   □ c. was greeted by a noisy crowd.

3. Some people feared that
   □ a. Lincoln would forget to come.
   □ b. someone would insult Lincoln.
   □ c. rain would spoil the occasion.

4. At this time, Lincoln was
   □ a. running for President.
   □ b. President-elect.
   □ c. President.

5. Lincoln was
   □ a. shaking hands and greeting people.
   □ b. anxious to get inside the Astor House.
   □ c. wearing black clothes.

Understanding the Passage

6. The narrator was
   □ a. one of Lincoln's critics.
   □ b. impressed by Lincoln.
   □ c. interested only in the crowd's reaction.

7. The most unusual aspect of the people in the crowd was their
   □ a. amazing attentiveness.
   □ b. quiet behavior.
   □ c. rapidly shifting moods.

8. To this crowd, Lincoln was
   □ a. a conquering hero.
   □ b. a promising young politician.
   □ c. something of a curiosity.

9. The narrator apparently
   □ a. had a fine view.
   □ b. knew Lincoln personally.
   □ c. both a and b.

10. Lincoln could best be described as
   □ a. calm and relaxed.
   □ b. unnerved by the crowd.
   □ c. preoccupied by his inauguration.

Among all the heroic faces which the painters of that age have preserved, none, perhaps, hardly excepting Shakespeare's or Spenser's, Alva's or Parma's, is more heroic than that of Richard Grenvil, as it stands in Prince's "Worthies of Devon"; of a Spanish type, perhaps (or more truly speaking, a Cornish), rather than an English, with just enough of the British element in it, to give delicacy to its massiveness. The forehead and whole brain are of extraordinary loftiness, and perfectly upright; the nose long, aquiline, and delicately pointed; the mouth fringed with a short silky beard, small and ripe, yet firm as granite, with just pout enough of the lower lip to give hint of that capacity of noble indignation which lay hid under its usual courtly calm and sweetness. If there be a defect in the face, it is that the eyes are somewhat small, and close together, and the eyebrows, though delicately arched, and without a trace of peevishness, too closely pressed down upon them. The complexion is dark, the figure tall and graceful; altogether the likeness of a wise and gallant gentleman, lovely to all good men, awful to all bad men; in whose presence none dare say or do a mean or a ribald thing; whom brave men left, feeling themselves nerved to do their duty better, while cowards slipped away, as bats and owls before the sun. So he lived and moved, whether in the court of Elizabeth, giving his counsel among the wisest; or in the streets of Bideford, capped alike by squire or merchant, shopkeeper and sailor; or riding along the moorland roads between his houses of Stow and Bideford, while every woman ran out to her door to look at the great Sir Richard, the pride of North Devon; or sitting there in the low mullioned window at Burrough, with his cup of malmsey before him, and the lute to which he had just been singing laid across his knees, while the red western sun streamed in upon his high, bland forehead, and soft curling locks; ever the same steadfast, God-fearing, chivalrous man, conscious of the pride of beauty, and strength, and valor, and wisdom, and a race and name which claimed direct descent from the grandfather of the Conqueror, and was tracked down the centuries by valiant deeds and noble benefits to his native shire, himself the noblest of his race.

Recalling Facts

1. The narrator found the painting of Richard Grenvil to be
   □ a. too British.
   □ b. indelicate.
   □ c. heroic.

2. Grenvil's nose was
   □ a. short.
   □ b. long.
   □ c. broken.

3. Grenvil's eyes were
   □ a. small and close together.
   □ b. big and menacing.
   □ c. sickly looking.

4. Grenvil served on the court of
   □ a. Bideford.
   □ b. Burrough.
   □ c. Elizabeth.

5. Grenvil was the pride of
   □ a. North Stow.
   □ b. South Bideford.
   □ c. North Devon.

Understanding the Passage

6. The face of Grenvil
   □ a. compared favorably with Spenser's.
   □ b. was inferior to both Alva and Parma.
   □ c. looked very much like Shakespeare's.

7. The painting's delicacy came from its
   □ a. massiveness.
   □ b. slight British touches.
   □ c. devotion to Spanish traditions.

8. Apparently, Grenvil was a man of considerable
   □ a. wisdom.
   □ b. kindness.
   □ c. both a and b.

9. In his day, Grenvil was
   □ a. well known to ordinary people.
   □ b. without political power.
   □ c. both a and b.

10. Grenvil came from a race of
    □ a. valiant and noble men.
    □ b. merchants and shopkeepers.
    □ c. oppressed people.

During the dread reign of cholera in New York, I had accepted the invitation of a relative to spend a fortnight with him in the retirement of his *cottage ornée* on the banks of the Hudson. We had here around us all the ordinary means of summer amusement; and what with rambling in the woods, sketching, boating, fishing, bathing, music, and books, we should have passed the time pleasantly enough, but for the fearful intelligence which reached up every morning from the populous city. Not a day elapsed which did not bring us news of the decease of some acquaintance. Then, as the fatality increased, we learned to expect daily the loss of some friend. At length we trembled at the approach of every messenger. The very air from the south seemed to us redolent with death. That palsying thought, indeed, took entire possession of my soul. I could neither speak, think, nor dream of anything else. My host was of a less excitable temperament, and, although greatly depressed in spirits, exerted himself to sustain my own. His richly philosophical intellect was not at any time affected by unrealities. To the substances of terror he was sufficiently alive, but of its shadows he had no apprehension.

His endeavors to arouse me were frustrated, in great measure, by certain volumes which I had found in his library. These were of a character to force into germination whatever seeds of hereditary superstition lay latent in my bosom. I had been reading these books without his knowledge, and thus he was often at a loss to account for the forcible impressions which had been made upon my fancy.

A favorite topic with me was the popular belief in omens—a belief which, at this one epoch in my life, I was almost seriously disposed to defend. On this subject we had long and animated discussions; he maintaining the utter groundlessness of faith in such matters, I contending that a popular sentiment arising with absolute spontaneity—that is to say, without apparent traces of suggestion—had in itself the unmistakable elements of truth, and was entitled to much respect.

The fact is, that soon after my arrival at the cottage there had occurred to myself an incident so entirely inexplicable, and which had in it so much of the portentous character, that I might well have been excused for regarding it as an omen.

Recalling Facts

1. The cottage was located on the banks of the
   - ☐ a. Missouri River.
   - ☐ b. Connecticut River.
   - ☐ c. Hudson River.

2. A fearful outbreak of cholera had struck
   - ☐ a. New York City.
   - ☐ b. Hartford, Connecticut.
   - ☐ c. Boston, Massachusetts.

3. The narrator read books about
   - ☐ a. architecture.
   - ☐ b. tropical diseases.
   - ☐ c. omens.

4. The narrator and his host often
   - ☐ a. traveled to the city together.
   - ☐ b. argued.
   - ☐ c. had the same dreams.

5. Shortly after the narrator arrived at the cottage,
   - ☐ a. something inexplicable happened.
   - ☐ b. he packed away all of his books.
   - ☐ c. both a and b.

Understanding the Passage

6. The narrator planned to stay with his friend
   - ☐ a. just one night.
   - ☐ b. for one weekend.
   - ☐ c. a couple of weeks.

7. Every day the narrator
   - ☐ a. went swimming and fishing.
   - ☐ b. received bad news.
   - ☐ c. longed to return to the city.

8. The cottage was located
   - ☐ a. south of the city.
   - ☐ b. north of the city.
   - ☐ c. east of the city.

9. The host can best be described as
   - ☐ a. irritable and demanding.
   - ☐ b. even tempered and rational.
   - ☐ c. superstitious and gloomy.

10. The narrator can best be described as
    - ☐ a. open-minded but fearful.
    - ☐ b. a cool intellectual.
    - ☐ c. a fearless daredevil.

Prince Vasili was not in the habit of forecasting his plans. Still less did he ever think of doing people harm for the sake of his own advantage. He was simply a man of the world, who had been successful in the world, so that success had become a sort of second nature to him. He was always accustomed to allow circumstances and his relations to other men to modify his various plans and projects; but he rarely gave himself a very scrupulous account of them, though they constituted his chief interest in life. He managed to have not merely one and not merely two, but a dozen, such plans and projects on the docket at one and the same time, and thus some only formulated themselves, some came to something, while others fell through.

He never said to himself, for example: "This man is now in my power, I ought to gain his confidence and friendship, and thereby secure myself the advantage of his assistance"; or this: "Here, Pierre is rich, I ought to induce him to marry my daughter, and thereby get the forty thousand rubles that I need." But if, by chance, he met the man in power, instinct immediately whispered to him that this man might be profitable to him, and Prince Vasili struck up a friendship with him, and at the first opportunity, led by instinct, flattered him, treated him with easy familiarity, and finally brought about the crucial conversation.

Pierre was under his tutelage at Moscow, and Prince Vasili procured for him an appointment as gentleman-in-waiting, which at that time conferred the same rank as Councillor of State, and he insisted on the young man accompanying him to Petersburg and taking up his residence in his own mansion.

Without making much effort, and at the same time taking it absolutely for granted that he was on the right track, Prince Vasili was doing everything in his power to marry Pierre to his daughter.

If Prince Vasili had devised his plans beforehand, he could not have been so natural in his conversation, so simple and unaffected in his relations with all men, not only those above him, but those who stood below him. There was something that ever attracted him to men richer or more powerful than himself, and he was endowed with the rare art of seizing just the right moment for profiting by people.

Recalling Facts

1. Prince Vasili rarely talked about his
   - ☐ a. friends.
   - ☐ b. projects.
   - ☐ c. past successes.

2. Prince Vasili was most influenced by
   - ☐ a. his instinct.
   - ☐ b. cold reasoning.
   - ☐ c. old friendships.

3. Prince Vasili insisted that Pierre come live with him in
   - ☐ a. Moscow.
   - ☐ b. Kiev.
   - ☐ c. Petersburg.

4. Prince Vasili wanted Pierre to
   - ☐ a. resign his post.
   - ☐ b. join in a business partnership.
   - ☐ c. marry his daughter.

5. In his conversations with other men, Prince Vasili was
   - ☐ a. relaxed.
   - ☐ b. anxious.
   - ☐ c. tongue-tied.

Understanding the Passage

6. Prince Vasili did not appear to be
   - ☐ a. an obvious manipulator.
   - ☐ b. an ambitious man.
   - ☐ c. a man with foresight.

7. It would be safe to say that
   - ☐ a. Prince Vasili was naive.
   - ☐ b. things came easily to Prince Vasili.
   - ☐ c. Prince Vasili lacked a formal education.

8. Prince Vasili could best be described as
   - ☐ a. greedy and rude.
   - ☐ b. cold and distant.
   - ☐ c. flexible and easygoing.

9. Apparently, Prince Vasili had an easy time
   - ☐ a. seeing all his projects through.
   - ☐ b. making influential friends.
   - ☐ c. both a and b.

10. Prince Vasili had a great sense of
    - ☐ a. romance.
    - ☐ b. independence.
    - ☐ c. timing.

28 *from* The Life and Adventures of Nicholas Nickleby *by Charles Dickens*

Both Mr. and Mrs. Squeers viewed the schoolboys in the light of their proper and natural enemies; or, in other words, they held and considered that their business and profession was to get as much from every boy as could by possibility be squeezed out of him. On this point they were both agreed, and behaved in unison accordingly. The only difference between them was that Mrs. Squeers waged war against the enemy openly and fearlessly, and that Squeers covered his rascality with a spice of his habitual deceit, as if he really had a notion of someday or other being able to take himself in, and persuade his own mind that he was a very good fellow.

Nicholas assisted his master to put on an old fustian shooting jacket, which he took down from a peg in the passage; and Squeers arming himself with his cane, led the way across a yard to a door in the rear of the schoolhouse.

The schoolhouse was such a crowded scene, and there were so many objects to attract attention, that at first Nicholas stared about him, really without seeing anything at all. By degrees, however, the place resolved itself into a bare and dirty room with a couple of windows, whereof a tenth part might be of glass, the remainder being stopped up with old copybooks and paper. There were a couple of long old rickety desks, cut and notched, and inked and damaged, in every possible way; two or three forms, a detached desk for Squeers, and another for his assistant. The ceiling was supported like that of a barn, by crossbeams and rafters, and the walls were so stained and discolored, that it was impossible to tell whether they had ever been touched with paint or whitewash.

But the pupils—the young noblemen! How the last faint traces of hope, the remotest glimmering of any good to be derived from his efforts in this den, faded from the mind of Nicholas as he looked in dismay around! Pale and haggard faces, lank and bony figures, children with the countenances of old men, deformities with irons upon their limbs, boys of stunted growth, and others whose long meager legs would hardly bear their stooping bodies, all crowded on the view together; there were the bleared eye, the harelip, the crooked foot, and every ugliness or distortion imaginable.

Reading Time _____ *Comprehension Score* _____ *Words per Minute* _____

Recalling Facts

1. Mr. and Mrs. Squeers ran a
   - ☐ a. workhouse.
   - ☐ b. schoolhouse.
   - ☐ c. prison.

2. Mr. Squeers was, by habit,
   - ☐ a. honorable.
   - ☐ b. meek.
   - ☐ c. deceitful.

3. Mr. Squeers carried a
   - ☐ a. cane.
   - ☐ b. gun.
   - ☐ c. umbrella.

4. The schoolhouse was
   - ☐ a. empty.
   - ☐ b. closed.
   - ☐ c. crowded.

5. Nicholas viewed the schoolhouse with
   - ☐ a. anticipation.
   - ☐ b. some hope.
   - ☐ c. dismay.

Understanding the Passage

6. Mr. and Mrs. Squeers can best be described as
   - ☐ a. conniving and unkind.
   - ☐ b. fair disciplinarians.
   - ☐ c. happily married.

7. Mr. Squeers liked to think that he was
   - ☐ a. a superior scholar.
   - ☐ b. really a nice person.
   - ☐ c. always praised by his students.

8. When Nicholas first stepped inside the school, he was
   - ☐ a. overwhelmed.
   - ☐ b. unimpressed.
   - ☐ c. expectant.

9. Mr. and Mrs. Squeers apparently did not
   - ☐ a. like their students.
   - ☐ b. know Nicholas.
   - ☐ c. care for each other.

10. The pupils can best be described as
    - ☐ a. academic underachievers.
    - ☐ b. unfortunate and unhealthy.
    - ☐ c. poor, but healthy.

from **Dr. Jekyll and Mr. Hyde** *by Robert Louis Stevenson*

I was born in the year 18-- to a large fortune, endowed besides with excellent parts, inclined by nature to industry, fond of the respect of the wise and good among my fellow men, and thus, as might have been supposed, with every guarantee of an honorable and distinguished future. And indeed the worst of my faults was a certain impatient gaiety of disposition, such as has made the happiness of many, but such as I found it hard to reconcile with my imperious desire to carry my head high, and wear a more than commonly grave countenance before the public. Hence it came about that I concealed my pleasures; and that when I reached years of reflection, and began to look round me and take stock of my progress and position in the world, I stood already committed to a profound duplicity of life. Many a man would have even blazoned such irregularities as I was guilty of; but from the high views that I had set before me, I regarded and hid them with an almost morbid sense of shame. It was thus rather the exacting nature of my aspirations than any particular degradation in my faults, that made me what I was, and, with even a deeper trench than in the majority of men, severed in me those provinces of good and ill which divide and compound man's dual nature. In this case, I was driven to reflect deeply and inveterately on that hard law of life, which lies at the root of religion and is one of the most plentiful springs of distress. Though so profound a double-dealer, I was in no sense a hypocrite; both sides of me were in dead earnest; I was no more myself when I laid aside restraint and plunged in shame, than when I labored, in the eye of day, at the furtherance of knowledge or the relief of sorrow and suffering. And it happened that the direction of my scientific studies, which led wholly towards the mystic and the transcendental, reacted and shed a strong light on this consciousness of the perennial war among my members. With every day, and from both sides of my intelligence, the moral and the intellectual, I thus drew steadily nearer to that truth, by whose partial discovery I have been doomed to such a dreadful shipwreck: that man is not truly one, but truly two.

*Reading Time*_____ *Comprehension Score*_____ *Words per Minute*_____ 71

Recalling Facts

1. The narrator was born into a
   - ☐ a. large family.
   - ☐ b. noble family.
   - ☐ c. wealthy family.

2. The narrator maintained that he was
   - ☐ a. a worthless human being.
   - ☐ b. not a hypocrite.
   - ☐ c. unique among men.

3. The narrator felt his worst fault was
   - ☐ a. his introspective thinking.
   - ☐ b. an impatient gaiety of disposition.
   - ☐ c. his mystic and transcendental leanings.

4. The narrator engaged in
   - ☐ a. many wild and public antics.
   - ☐ b. scientific studies.
   - ☐ c. romancing young ladies.

5. The narrator believed that every man
   - ☐ a. is doomed to self-destruction.
   - ☐ b. has a dual nature.
   - ☐ c. is responsible for the actions of others.

Understanding the Passage

6. The narrator
   - ☐ a. set high standards for himself.
   - ☐ b. had no ambition.
   - ☐ c. thought himself to be perfect.

7. The narrator was ashamed of his
   - ☐ a. wealth and education.
   - ☐ b. desire to alleviate suffering.
   - ☐ c. secret pleasures.

8. It seems the narrator spent a good deal of time engaged in
   - ☐ a. self-analysis.
   - ☐ b. leisure activities.
   - ☐ c. criticizing others.

9. The narrator believed he had an uncommonly deep split between
   - ☐ a. the goodness in him and the evil in him.
   - ☐ b. his desire to be rich and his desire to be a common man.
   - ☐ c. his hope for world peace and his hope for perennial war.

10. During the day, the narrator was apparently
   - ☐ a. an outcast.
   - ☐ b. a well-respected person.
   - ☐ c. a normal craftsman.

The studio was filled with the rich odor of roses, and when the light summer wind stirred amidst the trees of the garden there came through the open door the heavy scent of lilac, or the more delicate perfume of pink-flowering thorn.

From the corner of the divan of Persian saddlebags on which he was lying, smoking, as was his custom, innumerable cigarettes, Lord Henry Wotton could just catch the gleam of the honey-sweet and honey-colored blossoms of a laburnum, whose tremulous branches seemed hardly able to bear the burden of a beauty so flamelike as theirs; and now and then the fantastic shadows of birds in flight flitted across the long tussore silk curtains that were stretched in front of the huge window, producing a kind of momentary Japanese effect, and making him think of those pallid jade-faced painters of Tokyo who, through the medium of an art that is necessarily immobile, seek to convey the sense of swiftness and motion. The sullen murmur of the bees shouldering their way through the long unmown grass, or circling with monotonous insistence round the dusty gilt horns of the straggling woodbine, seemed to make the stillness more oppressive. The dim roar of London was like the bass note of a distant organ.

In the center of the room, clamped to an upright easel, stood the full-length portrait of a young man of extraordinary personal beauty, and in front of it, some little distance away, was sitting the artist himself, Basil Hallward, whose sudden disappearance some years ago caused, at the time, such public excitement, and gave rise to so many strange conjectures.

As the painter looked at the gracious and comely form he had so skill-fully mirrored in his art, a smile of pleasure passed across his face, and seemed about to linger there. But he suddenly started up, and, closing his eyes, placed his fingers upon the lids, as though he sought to imprison within his brain some curious dream from which he feared he might awake.

"It is your best work, Basil, the best thing you have ever done," said Lord Henry, languidly. "You must certainly send it next year to the Grosvenor—the Academy is too large and too vulgar—the Grosvenor is really the only place."

"I don't think I shall send it anywhere," Basil answered, tossing his head back in that odd way that made his friends laugh.

Recalling Facts

1. The studio was filled with the scent of
   - ☐ a. roses.
   - ☐ b. evergreens.
   - ☐ c. apple blossoms.

2. Lord Henry Wotton was accustomed to
   - ☐ a. taking long afternoon naps.
   - ☐ b. absolute solitude.
   - ☐ c. chain-smoking cigarettes.

3. In the background, Wotton could hear
   - ☐ a. the sounds of the city of London.
   - ☐ b. a siren wailing.
   - ☐ c. a mother calling her child.

4. Basil Hallward had just painted a
   - ☐ a. landscape scene.
   - ☐ b. still life painting.
   - ☐ c. full-length portrait.

5. Henry thought the painting should be displayed at the
   - ☐ a. Academy.
   - ☐ b. Grosvenor.
   - ☐ c. London Gallery of Art.

Understanding the Passage

6. The garden outside the studio was apparently
   - ☐ a. overrun with weeds.
   - ☐ b. quite beautiful.
   - ☐ c. the largest one in the neighborhood.

7. Lord Henry Wotton appeared to be quite
   - ☐ a. anxious.
   - ☐ b. comfortable.
   - ☐ c. unimpressed.

8. Basil Hallward was
   - ☐ a. a well-known artist.
   - ☐ b. an obscure artist.
   - ☐ c. a retired artist.

9. Hallward had apparently done
   - ☐ a. a masterful job with the painting.
   - ☐ b. paintings of this same subject before.
   - ☐ c. copies of this painting for several friends.

10. Basil Hallward did not think
    - ☐ a. Lord Henry's compliment was sincere.
    - ☐ b. he wanted to display the portrait anywhere.
    - ☐ c. the Academy was at all vulgar.

"Squire" Hawkins got his title from being postmaster of Obedstown—not that the title properly belonged to the office, but because in those regions the chief citizens always must have titles of some sort, and so the usual courtesy had been extended to Hawkins. The mail was monthly, and sometimes amounted to as much as three or four letters at a single delivery. Even a rush like this did not fill up the postmaster's whole month, though, and therefore he "kept store" in the intervals.

The Squire was contemplating the morning. It was balmy and tranquil; the vagrant breezes were laden with the odor of flowers; the murmur of bees was in the air; there was everywhere that suggestion of repose that summer woodlands bring to the senses, and the vague pleasurable melancholy that such a time and such surroundings inspire.

Presently the United States mail arrived, on horseback. There was but one letter, and it was for the postmaster. The long-legged youth who carried the mail tarried an hour to talk, for there was no hurry, and in a little while the male population of the village had assembled to help. As a general thing, they were dressed in homespun "jeans," blue or yellow—there were not other varieties of it; all wore one suspender and sometimes two—yarn ones which were knitted at home—some wore vests, but few wore coats. Such coats and vests as did appear, however, were rather picturesque than otherwise, for they were made of tolerably fanciful patterns of *calico*—a fashion which prevails there to this day among those of the community who have tastes above the common level and are able to afford style. Every individual arrived with his hands in his pockets; a hand came out occasionally for a purpose, but it always went back again after service; and if it was the head that was served, just the cant that the dilapidated straw hat got by being uplifted and rooted under was retained until the next call altered the inclination; many hats were present, but none were erect and no two were canted just alike. We are speaking impartially of men, youths, and boys; we are also speaking of these three estates when we say that every individual was either chewing natural leaf tobacco prepared on his own premises, or smoking the same in a corncob pipe.

*Reading Time*_____ *Comprehension Score*_____ *Words per Minute*_____   75

Recalling Facts

1. The title of "Squire" was
   - ☐ a. afforded to postmasters.
   - ☐ b. given as a courtesy.
   - ☐ c. passed down by Hawkins's father.

2. The mail arrived in Obedstown once a
   - ☐ a. day.
   - ☐ b. week.
   - ☐ c. month.

3. The mail was brought
   - ☐ a. on horseback.
   - ☐ b. by stagecoach.
   - ☐ c. by train.

4. The new batch of mail consisted of
   - ☐ a. one letter.
   - ☐ b. five letters.
   - ☐ c. fifty letters.

5. The narrator referred to men, youths, and boys as the three
   - ☐ a. stages.
   - ☐ b. periods.
   - ☐ c. estates.

Understanding the Passage

6. Obedstown must have been
   - ☐ a. a medium-sized city.
   - ☐ b. a huge metropolis.
   - ☐ c. an isolated settlement.

7. This scene took place during the
   - ☐ a. fall.
   - ☐ b. spring.
   - ☐ c. summer.

8. The letter carrier
   - ☐ a. was in a hurry.
   - ☐ b. had time to spare.
   - ☐ c. needed an assistant.

9. The men in town seemed to
   - ☐ a. have plenty of free time.
   - ☐ b. be too busy to notice the letter carrier.
   - ☐ c. be personal friends of the letter carrier.

10. Being the postmaster of Obedstown was
    - ☐ a. a full-time job.
    - ☐ b. not a very time-consuming job.
    - ☐ c. the most interesting job in town.

Mr. Wentworth, though he went punctiliously to call upon her, was not able to feel that he was getting used to his niece. It taxed his imagination to believe that she was really his half-sister's child. His sister was a figure of his early years; she had been only twenty when she went abroad, never to return, making in foreign parts a willful and undesirable marriage. His aunt, who had taken her to Europe for the benefit of the tour, gave, on her return, so lamentable an account of Mr. Adolphus Young, to whom the headstrong girl had united her destiny, that it operated as a chill upon family feeling—especially in the case of the half-brothers. Catherine had done nothing subsequently to propitiate her family; she had not even written to them in a way that indicated a lucid appreciation of their suspended sympathy, so that it had become a tradition in Boston circles that the highest charity, as regards this young lady, was to think it well to forget her, and to abstain from conjecture as to the extent to which her aberrations were reproduced in her descendants. Over these young people—a vague report of their existence had come to his ears—Mr. Wentworth had not, in the course of years, allowed his imagination to hover. Now that his nephew and niece had come before him, he perceived that they were the fruit of influences and circumstances very different from those under which his own familiar progeny had reached a vaguely qualified maturity. He felt no provocation to say that these influences had been exerted for evil; but he was sometimes afraid that he should not be able to like his distinguished, delicate, ladylike niece. He was paralyzed and bewildered by her foreignness. She spoke, somehow, a different language. There was something strange in her words. He had a feeling that another man, in his place, would accommodate himself to her tone; would ask her questions and joke with her, reply to those pleasantries of her own which sometimes seemed startling as addressed to an uncle. But Mr. Wentworth could not do these things. He could not even bring himself to attempt to measure her position in the world. She was the wife of a foreign nobleman who desired to repudiate her. This had a singular sound, but the old man felt himself destitute of the materials for a judgment.

Recalling Facts

1. Mr. Wentworth's half-sister was only twenty when she
   - □ a. went abroad.
   - □ b. left school.
   - □ c. lost her job.

2. Mr. Adolphus Young was the half-sister's
   - □ a. teacher.
   - □ b. tour guide.
   - □ c. husband.

3. Mr. Wentworth felt bewildered by his niece's
   - □ a. aggressiveness.
   - □ b. lack of education.
   - □ c. foreignness.

4. Mr. Wentworth's niece was married to a
   - □ a. foreign nobleman.
   - □ b. business tycoon.
   - □ c. language teacher.

5. The niece's husband wanted to
   - □ a. bring her to America.
   - □ b. care for her.
   - □ c. repudiate her.

Understanding the Passage

6. Mr. Wentworth's family did not approve of Catherine's
   - □ a. touring Europe.
   - □ b. marrying Mr. Young.
   - □ c. having children.

7. Mr. Wentworth felt
   - □ a. uncomfortable around his niece.
   - □ b. great love for his niece.
   - □ c. remorse over neglecting Catherine.

8. Mr. Wentworth felt that his own children were
   - □ a. very different from his niece.
   - □ b. prepared to like his niece.
   - □ c. too busy to visit their cousin.

9. Mr. Wentworth had never spent much time
   - □ a. thinking about his niece and nephew.
   - □ b. with his own children.
   - □ c. in Boston.

10. Mr. Wentworth felt that most men would be
    - □ a. upset if their sisters moved to Europe.
    - □ b. unwilling to visit a niece.
    - □ c. more at ease with a niece than he was.

The writer of these veracious pages was once walking through a splendid English palace standing amidst parks and gardens, than which none more magnificent has been since the days of Aladdin, in company with a melancholy friend, who viewed all things darkly through his gloomy eyes. The housekeeper, pattering on before us from chamber to chamber, was expatiating upon the magnificence of this picture; the beauty of that statue; the marvelous richness of these hangings and carpets; the admirable likeness of the late Marquis by Sir Thomas; of his father the fifth Earl, by Sir Joshua, and so on; when, in the very richest room of the whole castle, Hicks—such was my melancholy companion's name—stopped the cicerone in her prattle, saying in a hollow voice, "And now, madam, will you show us the closet *where the skeleton is?*" The scared functionary paused in the midst of her harangue; that article was not inserted in the catalogue which she daily utters to visitors for their half crown. Hick's question brought a darkness down upon the hall where we were standing. We did not see the room: and yet I have no doubt there is such a one; and ever after, when I have thought of the splendid castle towering in the midst of shady trees, under which the dappled deer are browsing; of the terraces gleaming with statues, and bright with a hundred thousand flowers; of the bridges and shining fountains and rivers wherein the castle windows reflect their festive gleams, when the halls are filled with happy feasters, and over the darkling woods comes the sound of music—always, I say, when I think of the Castle Bluebeard, it is to think of that dark little closet, which I know is there, and which the lordly owner opens shuddering—after midnight—when he is sleepless and *must* go unlock it, when the palace is hushed and beauties are sleeping around him unconscious, and revelers are at rest.

Have we not all such closets, my jolly friend, as well as the noble Marquis of Carabras? At night, when all the house is asleep but you, don't you get up and peep into yours? When you in your turn are slumbering, up gets your wife from your side, steals downstairs to her ghoul, clicks open the secret door, and looks into *her* dark depository. Psha! Who knows anyone save himself alone?

Recalling Facts

1. Hicks was
   - ☐ a. depressed.
   - ☐ b. anxious.
   - ☐ c. cheerful.

2. The likeness of the late Marquis was done by
   - ☐ a. the fifth earl.
   - ☐ b. Sir Joshua.
   - ☐ c. Sir Thomas.

3. The "cicerone" refers to the
   - ☐ a. housekeeper.
   - ☐ b. palace.
   - ☐ c. carpet.

4. The cost of the tour was
   - ☐ a. one dollar.
   - ☐ b. a half crown.
   - ☐ c. one pound.

5. The narrator believes that all people have something hidden in their
   - ☐ a. attic.
   - ☐ b. garage.
   - ☐ c. closet.

Understanding the Passage

6. The narrator regarded the palace grounds as
   - ☐ a. melancholy.
   - ☐ b. splendid.
   - ☐ c. commonplace.

7. Hicks can best be described as a
   - ☐ a. cynic.
   - ☐ b. bore.
   - ☐ c. critic.

8. Hicks's question about the closet
   - ☐ a. upset the narrator.
   - ☐ b. surprised the guide.
   - ☐ c. exposed the hiding place.

9. The narrator assumes that everyone has
   - ☐ a. something to hide.
   - ☐ b. many sleepless nights.
   - ☐ c. an appreciation for beautiful old castles.

10. After Hicks's comment, the narrator could not think of the castle without thinking of
   - ☐ a. the skeleton in the closet.
   - ☐ b. Bluebeard's ghost.
   - ☐ c. the flustered housekeeper.

What sort of a man was Wakefield? We are free to shape out our own idea and call it by his name. He was now in the meridian of life; his matrimonial affections, never violent, were sobered into a calm, habitual sentiment; of all husbands, he was likely to be the most constant, because a certain sluggishness would keep his heart at rest, wherever it might be placed. He was intellectual but not actively so; his mind occupied itself in long and lazy musings, that ended to no purpose, or had not vigor to attain it; his thoughts were seldom so energetic as to seize hold of words. Imagination, in the proper meaning of the term, made no part of Wakefield's gifts. With a cold but not depraved nor wandering heart, and a mind never feverish with riotous thoughts, nor perplexed with originality, who could have anticipated that our friend would entitle himself to a foremost place among the doers of eccentric deeds? Had his acquaintances been asked who was the man in London the surest to perform nothing today which should be remembered on the morrow, they would have thought of Wakefield. Only the wife of his bosom might have hesitated. She, without having analyzed his character, was partly aware of a quiet selfishness that had rusted into his inactive mind; of a peculiar sort of vanity, the most uneasy attribute about him; of a disposition to craft, which had seldom produced more positive effects than the keeping of petty secrets, hardly worth revealing; and, lastly, of what she called a little strangeness, sometimes, in the good man. This latter quality is indefinable and perhaps nonexistent.

Let us now imagine Wakefield bidding adieu to his wife. It is the dusk of an October evening. His equipment is a drab greatcoat, a hat covered with an oilcloth, top boots, an umbrella in one hand and a small portmanteau in the other. He has informed Mrs. Wakefield that he is to take the night coach into the country. She would fain inquire the length of his journey, its object, and the probable time of his return; but, indulgent to his harmless love of mystery, interrogates him only by a look. He tells her not to expect him positively by the return coach, nor to be alarmed should he tarry three or four days; but, at all events, to look for him on Friday evening.

Recalling Facts

1. Wakefield lacked
   - ☐ a. intelligence.
   - ☐ b. imagination.
   - ☐ c. integrity.

2. Wakefield's heart was described as
   - ☐ a. cold.
   - ☐ b. wandering.
   - ☐ c. depraved.

3. Wakefield lived in
   - ☐ a. New York.
   - ☐ b. Liverpool.
   - ☐ c. London.

4. Wakefield told his wife he might be gone for three or four
   - ☐ a. hours.
   - ☐ b. days.
   - ☐ c. weeks.

5. Wakefield told his wife to expect him back by
   - ☐ a. sunset.
   - ☐ b. Sunday morning.
   - ☐ c. Friday night.

Understanding the Passage

6. Wakefield can best be described as
   - ☐ a. wild and impetuous.
   - ☐ b. dull and predictable.
   - ☐ c. emotional and creative.

7. Wakefield appeared to be uninterested in
   - ☐ a. other women.
   - ☐ b. his wife.
   - ☐ c. his surroundings.

8. No one thought that Wakefield would turn out to be
   - ☐ a. an eccentric.
   - ☐ b. a success.
   - ☐ c. a dedicated husband.

9. Wakefield's wife detected in him some
   - ☐ a. deep religious feelings.
   - ☐ b. devious thoughts.
   - ☐ c. selfish vanity.

10. Wakefield's wife did not
   - ☐ a. speak to Wakefield while he was home.
   - ☐ b. demand to know Wakefield's exact schedule.
   - ☐ c. let her husband leave for the country.

Once in the autumn I happened to be in a very unpleasant and inconvenient position. In the town where I had just arrived and where I knew not a soul, I found myself without a farthing in my pocket and without a night's lodging.

Having sold during the first few days every part of my costume without which it was still possible to go about, I passed from the town into the quarter called "Yste," where were the steamship wharves—a quarter which during the navigation season fermented with boisterous, laborious life, but now was silent and deserted, for we were in the last days of October.

Dragging my feet along the moist sand, and obstinately scrutinizing it with the desire to discover in it any sort of fragment of food, I wandered alone among the deserted buildings and warehouses, and thought how good it would be to get a full meal.

In our present state of culture hunger of the mind is more quickly satisfied than hunger of the body. You wander about the streets, you are surrounded by buildings not bad looking from the outside and—you may safely say it—not so badly furnished inside, and the sight of them may excite within you stimulating ideas about architecture, hygiene, and many other wise and high-flying subjects. You may meet warmly and neatly dressed folks—all very polite, and turning away from you tactfully, not wishing offensively to notice the lamentable fact of your existence. Well, well, the mind of a hungry man is always better nourished and healthier than the mind of the well-fed man; and there you have a situation from which you may draw a very ingenious conclusion in favor of the ill-fed.

The evening was approaching, the rain was falling, and the wind blew violently from the north. It whistled in the empty booths and shops, blew into the plastered windowpanes of the taverns, and whipped into foam the wavelets of the river which splashed noisily on the sandy shore, casting high their white crests, racing one after another into the dim distance, and leaping impetuously over one another's shoulders. It seemed as if the river felt the proximity of winter, and was running at random away from the fetters of ice which the north wind might well have flung upon her that very night. The sky was heavy and dark.

Recalling Facts

1. Yste was a
   ☐ a. section of town.
   ☐ b. steamship.
   ☐ c. rundown hotel.

2. This scene took place during the last days of
   ☐ a. winter.
   ☐ b. October.
   ☐ c. the festival season.

3. The area of Yste was
   ☐ a. extremely shabby.
   ☐ b. crowded with people.
   ☐ c. deserted.

4. As evening approached,
   ☐ a. the wind blew violently.
   ☐ b. the snow stopped falling.
   ☐ c. both a and b.

5. The town was located
   ☐ a. in the mountains.
   ☐ b. on a river.
   ☐ c. near the ocean.

Understanding the Passage

6. The narrator talked about a situation where he was
   ☐ a. hopeful.
   ☐ b. desperate.
   ☐ c. furious.

7. The narrator had recently got some money by
   ☐ a. begging in the streets.
   ☐ b. selling his clothes.
   ☐ c. working on the wharves.

8. The population of the town
   ☐ a. had grown recently.
   ☐ b. varied greatly with the seasons.
   ☐ c. was unusually well educated.

9. The narrator appeared to be
   ☐ a. well educated.
   ☐ b. angry at the world.
   ☐ c. unable to think of anything but food.

10. The wind
   ☐ a. made the air feel colder.
   ☐ b. cheered the narrator.
   ☐ c. stopped suddenly.

At first Felice had been, for Lockwood, a pretty woman, neither more nor less; but by degrees she emerged from this vague classification: she became a very pretty woman. Then she became a personality; she occupied a place within the circle which Lockwood called his world, his life. For the past months this place had to be enlarged. Lockwood allowed it to expand— encouraged it to expand. To make room for Felice, he thrust aside, or allowed the idea of Felice to thrust aside, other objects which long had sat secure. The invasion of the woman into the sphere of his existence developed into a thing veritably headlong. Deep-seated convictions, old established beliefs and ideals, even the two landmarks right and wrong, were hustled and shouldered about as the invasion widened and penetrated. This state of affairs was further complicated by the fact that Felice was the wife of Chino Zavalla, shift boss of No. 4 gang in the new workings.

It was quite possible that though Lockwood could not have told when and how the acquaintance between him and Felice began and progressed, the young woman herself could. But this is guesswork. Felice being a woman, and part Spanish at that, was vastly more self-conscious, more disingenuous, than the man. Also she had that fearlessness that very pretty women have. In her more refined and city-bred sisters this fearlessness would be called poise, or, at the most, self-assurance. In Felice it was audacity, or, at the most, "cheek." And she was quite capable of making young Lockwood, the superintendent, her employer, and nominally the ruler of her little world, fall in love with her. It is only fair to Felice to say that she would not do this deliberately. She would be more conscious of the business than the man, than Lockwood; but in affairs such as this involving women like Felice there is a distinction between deliberately doing a thing and consciously doing it. Admittedly this is complicated, but it must be understood that Felice herself was complex, and she could no more help attracting men to her than the magnet the steel filings. It made no difference whether the man was the "breed" boy who split logging down by the engine house or the young superintendent with his college education, his delicate white hands, and dominating position: Felice had influence over each and all who came within her range.

Recalling Facts

1. Felice was married to
   - ☐ a. Lockwood.
   - ☐ b. Chino.
   - ☐ c. no one.

2. Felice was part
   - ☐ a. Irish.
   - ☐ b. Italian.
   - ☐ c. Spanish.

3. Felice was known for her
   - ☐ a. beauty.
   - ☐ b. fearfulness.
   - ☐ c. both a and b.

4. "Cheek" refers to
   - ☐ a. a kind of self-assurance.
   - ☐ b. the shift boss of a mine.
   - ☐ c. anyone with Spanish blood.

5. Lockwood was
   - ☐ a. a shift boss.
   - ☐ b. an extremely wealthy man.
   - ☐ c. a superintendent.

Understanding the Passage

6. Lockwood fell in love with Felice
   - ☐ a. at first sight.
   - ☐ b. over time.
   - ☐ c. to spite Chino.

7. Lockwood's love of Felice
   - ☐ a. superceded his old passions.
   - ☐ b. led to easier promotions.
   - ☐ c. devastated his wife.

8. Seemingly, the person most aware of the developing friendship was
   - ☐ a. Felice.
   - ☐ b. Lockwood.
   - ☐ c. Chino.

9. Felice had almost no control over her
   - ☐ a. ability to attract men.
   - ☐ b. daydreams.
   - ☐ c. husband and children.

10. Apparently, Felice and Lockwood
   - ☐ a. had similar educational backgrounds.
   - ☐ b. knew how to live in the city.
   - ☐ c. came from different social classes.

The sun, by which the knight had chiefly directed his course, had now sunk behind the Derbyshire hills on his left, and every effort which he might take to pursue his journey was as likely to lead him out of his road as to advance him on his route. After having in vain endeavored to select the most beaten path in hopes it might lead to the cottage of some herdsman, or the sylvan lodge of a forester, and having repeatedly found himself totally unable to determine on a choice, the knight resolved to trust to the sagacity of his horse; experience having, on former occasions, made him acquainted with the wonderful talent possessed by these animals for extricating themselves and their riders on such emergencies.

The good steed, grievously fatigued with so long a day's journey under a rider cased in mail, had no sooner found, by the slackened reins, that he was abandoned to his own guidance, than he seemed to assume new strength and spirit; and whereas formerly he had scarce replied to the spur, otherwise than by a groan, he now, as if proud of the confidence reposed in him, pricked up his ears, and assumed, of his own accord, a more lively motion. The path which the animal adopted rather turned off from the course pursued by the knight during the day; but as the horse seemed confident in his choice, the rider abandoned himself to his discretion.

He was justified by the event; for the footpath soon after appeared a little wider and more worn, and the tinkle of a small bell gave the knight to understand that he was in the vicinity of some chapel or hermitage.

Accordingly, he soon reached an open plat of turf, on the opposite side of which a rock, rising abruptly from a gently sloping plain, offered its grey and weather-beaten front to the traveler. Ivy mantled its sides in some places, and in others oaks and holly bushes, whose roots found nourishment in the cliffs of the crag, waved over the precipices below, like the plumage of the warrior over his steel helmet, giving grace to that whose chief expression was terror. At the bottom of the rock was constructed a rude hut, built chiefly of the trunks of trees felled in the neighboring forest, and secured against the weather by having its crevices stuffed with moss mingled with clay.

*Reading Time*_____ *Comprehension Score*_____ *Words per Minute*_____   87

Recalling Facts

1. During the day, the knight directed his course by
   ☐ a. following the sun.
   ☐ b. using the wind.
   ☐ c. following a broad road.

2. The knight finally
   ☐ a. made camp.
   ☐ b. let his horse choose the course.
   ☐ c. found a herdsman's cottage.

3. The knight was
   ☐ a. lost.
   ☐ b. cased in mail.
   ☐ c. both a and b.

4. The first sound of civilization the knight heard was the
   ☐ a. tinkle of a bell.
   ☐ b. crackle of a wood fire.
   ☐ c. sound of muffled gunshots.

5. The rude hut was built chiefly from
   ☐ a. pine logs.
   ☐ b. stones.
   ☐ c. trunks of trees.

Understanding the Passage

6. By the day's end, the knight was
   ☐ a. rather frustrated.
   ☐ b. worn out by battle.
   ☐ c. suffering from sunstroke.

7. The knight's horse had
   ☐ a. an ability to find a beaten path.
   ☐ b. no instincts of its own.
   ☐ c. eagerly responded to its rider's every command.

8. The confidence placed in the horse by the knight
   ☐ a. went unnoticed.
   ☐ b. enlivened the horse.
   ☐ c. led to disaster.

9. The path chosen by the horse was
   ☐ a. one that went around in a circle.
   ☐ b. a poor choice.
   ☐ c. a good choice.

10. The knight wanted to find
    ☐ a. the battlefield.
    ☐ b. other knights.
    ☐ c. anyone at all.

Clym and Eustacia Yeobright, in their little house at Alderworth, beyond East Egdon, were living on with a monotony which was positively delightful to them. The heath and changes of weather were quite blotted out from their eyes for the present. They were enclosed in a sort of luminous mist, which hid from them surroundings of any inharmonious color, and gave to all things the character of light. When it rained they were charmed, because they could remain indoors together all day with such a show of reason; when it was fine they were charmed, because they could sit together on the hills. They were like those double stars which revolve around and around each other, and from a distance appear to be one. The absolute solitude in which they lived intensified their reciprocal thoughts; yet some might have speculated that it had the disadvantage of consuming their mutual affection at a fearfully prodigal rate. Yeobright did not fear for his own part; but recollection of Eustacia's old speech about the evanescence of love, now apparently forgotten by her, sometimes caused him to ask himself a question; and he recoiled at the thought that the quality of finiteness was not foreign to Eden.

When three or four weeks had been passed thus, Yeobright resumed his reading in earnest. To make up for lost time he studied indefatigably, for he wished to enter his new profession with the least possible delay.

Now, Eustacia's dream had always been that, once married to Clym, she would have the power of inducing him to return to Paris. He had carefully withheld all promise to do so; but would he be proof against her coaxing and argument? She had calculated to such a degree on the probability of success that she had represented Paris, and not Budmouth, to her grandfather as in all likelihood their future home. Her hopes were bound up in this dream. In the quiet days since their marriage, when Yeobright had been poring over her lips, her eyes, and the lines of her face, she had mused and mused on the subject, even while in the act of returning his gaze; and now the sight of the books, indicating his intention to stick to his plan of opening an innovative school in the rural village of Budmouth—a future which was antagonistic to her dream—struck her with a positively painful jar.

Recalling Facts

1. Clym and Eustacia were
   currently living in
   □ a. Paris.
   □ b. Alderworth.
   □ c. London.

2. After three or four weeks,
   Clym began to resume his
   □ a. farming.
   □ b. traveling.
   □ c. studying.

3. Eustacia desperately wanted
   Clym to return to
   □ a. Budmouth.
   □ b. East Egdon.
   □ c. Paris.

4. Clym wanted to
   □ a. open an innovative school.
   □ b. become a country doctor.
   □ c. take over the family
       business.

5. Clym was eager to
   □ a. start his new profession.
   □ b. begin a family.
   □ c. have Eustacia
       begin working.

Understanding the Passage

6. Clym and Eustacia were
   □ a. cousins.
   □ b. newlyweds.
   □ c. unhappy.

7. Clym had made
   □ a. no false promises
       to Eustacia.
   □ b. an enemy of Eustacia's
       grandfather.
   □ c. a mistake in focusing on
       the village of Budmouth.

8. Eustacia had great confidence in her ability to
   □ a. influence Clym.
   □ b. travel alone to Paris.
   □ c. change her grand-
       father's mind.

9. Clym feared that Eustacia's
   love for him would
   □ a. make other men jealous.
   □ b. overpower him.
   □ c. eventually fade.

10. Clym and Eustacia seemed
    to have
    □ a. no sense of how
        to manage money.
    □ b. different plans for
        their life together.
    □ c. many friends in
        the area.

Ishmael Bush had passed the whole of a life of more than fifty years on the skirts of society. He boasted that he had never dwelt where he might not safely fell every tree he could view from his own threshold; that the law had rarely been known to enter his clearing; and that his ears had never willingly admitted the sound of a church bell. His exertions seldom exceeded his wants, which were peculiar to his class, and rarely failed of being supplied. He had no respect for any learning, except that of the leech, because he was ignorant of the application of any other intelligence than such as met the senses. His deference to this particular branch of science had induced him to listen to a medical man, whose thirst of natural history had led him to the desire of profiting by the migratory propensities of the squatter. This gentleman he had received into his family, or rather under his protection. They had journeyed together thus far through the prairies, in perfect harmony: Ishmael often felicitating his wife on the possession of a companion, who would be so helpful in their new abode, wherever it might chance to be, until the family were thoroughly "acclimated." The pursuits of the naturalist frequently led him, however, for days at a time, from the direct line of the route of the squatter, who rarely seemed to have any other guide than the sun. Most men would have deemed themselves fortunate to have been absent on the perilous occasion of the Sioux inroad, as was Obed Bat (or, as he was fond of hearing himself called, Battius), M.D., and fellow of several learned societies— the adventurous gentleman in question.

Although the sluggish nature of Ishmael was not actually awakened, it was sorely pricked by the liberties which had just been taken with his property. He slept, however, for it was the hour he had allotted to that refreshment, and because he knew how impotent any exertions to recover his effects must prove in the darkness of midnight. He also knew the danger of his present position too well to hazard what was left, in pursuit of that which was lost. Much as the inhabitants of the prairie were known to love horses, their attachment to many other articles, still in the possession of the travelers, was equally well understood.

Recalling Facts

1. Ishmael Bush had no respect for
   - ☐ a. the wilderness.
   - ☐ b. formal learning.
   - ☐ c. tree cutters.

2. Ishmael was a
   - ☐ a. logger.
   - ☐ b. trapper.
   - ☐ c. squatter.

3. Battius was one name of
   - ☐ a. the medical man.
   - ☐ b. Ishmael Bush.
   - ☐ c. Ishmael's wife.

4. Ishmael was usually guided by
   - ☐ a. the sun.
   - ☐ b. the stars.
   - ☐ c. an old map.

5. Ishmael was prevented from trying to recover his property by
   - ☐ a. hunger.
   - ☐ b. his wife.
   - ☐ c. darkness.

Understanding the Passage

6. Ishmael enjoyed living
   - ☐ a. near a town.
   - ☐ b. in the wilderness.
   - ☐ c. where there was law and order.

7. Ishmael appeared to be
   - ☐ a. self-sufficient.
   - ☐ b. dependent on Obed Bat.
   - ☐ c. unhappy with his wife.

8. Ishmael had not spent much time in
   - ☐ a. church.
   - ☐ b. school.
   - ☐ c. both a and b.

9. Ishmael
   - ☐ a. knew most of the Sioux on the prairie.
   - ☐ b. disturbed Obed Bat from the beginning.
   - ☐ c. was looking for a place to settle.

10. Obed Bat liked to study
    - ☐ a. the lifestyle of squatters.
    - ☐ b. architecture.
    - ☐ c. nature.

Among the devoted supporters of amateur theatricals and concerts for charitable objects, the Azhogins, who lived in their own house in Great Dvoryansky Street, took a prominent place. They always provided the room, and took upon themselves all the troublesome arrangements and the expenses. They were a family of wealthy landowners who had an estate of some nine thousand acres in the district and a capital house, but they did not care for the country, and lived winter and summer alike in the town. The family consisted of the mother, a tall, thin, refined lady, with short hair, a short jacket, and a flat-looking skirt in the English fashion, and three daughters who, when they were spoken of, were called not by their names but simply: the eldest, the middle, and the youngest. They were dressed like their mother; they lisped disagreeably and yet, in spite of that, infallibly took part in every performance and were continually doing something with a charitable object—acting, reciting, singing. They were very serious and never smiled, and even in a musical comedy they played without the faintest trace of gaiety.

I loved our theatricals, especially the numerous, noisy, and rather incoherent rehearsals, after which they always gave a supper. In the choice of the plays and the distribution of the parts I had no hand at all. The post assigned to me lay behind the scenes. I painted the scenes, copied out the parts, prompted, made up the actors' faces; and I was entrusted, too, with various stage effects such as thunder, the singing of nightingales, and so on. Since I had no proper social position and no decent clothes, at the rehearsals I held aloof from the rest in the shadows of the wings and maintained a shy silence.

I painted the scenes at the Azhogins' either in the barn or the yard. I was assisted by Andrey Ivanov, a house painter, or, as he called himself, a contractor for all kinds of house decorations, a tall, very thin, pale man of fifty, with a hollow chest, with sunken temples, with blue rings round his eyes, rather terrible to look at in fact. He was afflicted with some internal malady, and every autumn and spring people said that he wouldn't recover, but after being laid up he would get up and say afterwards with surprise: "I have escaped dying again."

Recalling Facts

1. The Azhogins were
   - ☐ a. stockbrokers.
   - ☐ b. wealthy landowners.
   - ☐ c. oil barons.

2. The Azhogins spent almost all their time
   - ☐ a. at their country estate.
   - ☐ b. traveling overseas.
   - ☐ c. in the town.

3. "The eldest, the middle, and the youngest" refers to the Azhogin
   - ☐ a. daughters.
   - ☐ b. sons.
   - ☐ c. grandchildren.

4. The narrator
   - ☐ a. was a part-time actor.
   - ☐ b. starred in musical comedies.
   - ☐ c. worked behind the scenes.

5. Andrey Ivanov was often
   - ☐ a. late for work.
   - ☐ b. sick.
   - ☐ c. used as an actor.

Understanding the Passage

6. The Azhogins were
   - ☐ a. generous with their time and money.
   - ☐ b. interested only in theatrical productions.
   - ☐ c. disinterested supporters of the arts.

7. The daughters were charitable but lacked
   - ☐ a. much free time.
   - ☐ b. real acting talent.
   - ☐ c. a serious attitude toward life.

8. The narrator apparently was
   - ☐ a. rather poor.
   - ☐ b. a wonderful actor.
   - ☐ c. both a and b.

9. The narrator could best be described as
   - ☐ a. an undiscovered talent.
   - ☐ b. resentful and bitter.
   - ☐ c. a jack-of-all-trades.

10. Andrey Ivanov continually surprised himself by his
   - ☐ a. painting accomplishments.
   - ☐ b. serious illnesses.
   - ☐ c. medical recoveries.

from **The Old Wives' Tale** *by Arnold Bennett*

It was after midnight when they went into the Restaurant Sylvain; Gerald, having decided not to go to the hotel, had changed his mind and called there, and having called there, had remained a long time. Sophia was already accustoming herself to the idea that, with Gerald, it was impossible to predict accurately more than five minutes of the future.

As the footman held open the door for them to enter, and Sophia passed modestly into the glowing yellow interior of the restaurant, followed by Gerald in his character of man of the world, they drew the attention of Sylvain's numerous and glittering guests. No face could have made a more provocative contrast to the women's faces in those screened rooms than the face of Sophia, so childlike between the baby's bonnet and the huge bow of ribbon, so candid, so charmingly conscious of its own pure beauty. She saw around her, clustered about the white tables, multitudes of violently red lips, powdered cheeks, cold, hard eyes, self-possessed arrogant faces, and insolent bosoms. What had impressed her more than anything else here in Paris, more even than the three-horsed omnibuses, was the extraordinary self-assurance of the women, their unashamed posing, their calm acceptance of the public gaze. They seemed to say: "We are the renowned Parisiennes." They frightened her: they appeared to her so corrupt and so proud in their corruption. She had already seen a dozen women in various situations of conspicuousness apply powder to their complexions with no more ado than if they had been giving a pat to their hair. She couldn't understand such boldness. As for them, they marveled at the phenomena presented in Sophia's person; they admired; they admitted the style of the gown; but they envied neither her innocence nor her beauty; they envied nothing but her youth and the fresh tint of her cheeks.

Gerald had a very curt way with waiters; and the more obsequious they were, the haughtier he became. A headwaiter was no more to him than a scullion. He gave loud-voiced orders in French of which both he and Sophia were proud, and a table was laid for them in a corner near one of the large windows. Sophia settled herself on the bench of green velvet and began to ply the ivory fan which Gerald had given her. It was very hot, and all the windows were open.

Recalling Facts

1. Gerald and Sophia arrived at
   the Restaurant Sylvain
   ☐ a. at five o'clock.
   ☐ b. just before ten o'clock.
   ☐ c. after midnight.

2. Sophia's face was described as
   ☐ a. childlike.
   ☐ b. undistinguished.
   ☐ c. noble.

3. In Paris, Sophia was most
   impressed by the
   ☐ a. self-assurance of
       the women.
   ☐ b. three-horsed omnibuses.
   ☐ c. quality of the
       restaurant food.

4. The Parisiennes wore
   ☐ a. a considerable amount
       of makeup.
   ☐ b. modest and conser-
       vative gowns.
   ☐ c. flowers and ribbons
       in their hair.

5. Gerald ordered in
   ☐ a. English.
   ☐ b. French.
   ☐ c. German.

Understanding the Passage

6. Sophia found Gerald
   ☐ a. highly unpredictable.
   ☐ b. shy and withdrawn.
   ☐ c. too sophisticated
       for her.

7. The customers at Sylvain
   ☐ a. scrutinized strangers.
   ☐ b. ignored foreigners.
   ☐ c. greeted Gerald warmly.

8. Apparently, the female
   customers at Sylvain's were
   ☐ a. down on their luck.
   ☐ b. rich and successful.
   ☐ c. modest wives
       and mothers.

9. Sophia was put off by
   the Parisiennes'
   ☐ a. overblown pride.
   ☐ b. lack of table manners.
   ☐ c. loud voices.

10. The Parisiennes did
    not admire
    ☐ a. innocence.
    ☐ b. a healthy complexion.
    ☐ c. youth.

It had been a year of strange disturbances—a desolating drought, a hurly-burly of destructive tempests, killing frosts in the tender valleys, mortal fevers in the tender homes. Now came tidings that all day the wail of myriads of locusts was heard in the green woods of Virginia and Tennessee; now that Lake Erie was blocked with ice on the very verge of summer, so that in the Niagara new rocks and islands showed their startling faces. In the bluegrass region of Kentucky countless caterpillars were crawling over the ripening apple orchards and leaving the trees as stark as when tossed in the thin air of bitter February days.

Then, flying low and heavily through drought and tempest and frost and plague, like the royal presence of disaster, that had been but heralded by its mournful train, came nearer and nearer the dark angel of the pestilence.

M. Xaupi had given a great ball only the night before in the dancing rooms over the confectionery of M. Giron—that M. Giron who made the tall pyramids of meringues and macaroons for wedding suppers, and spun around them a cloud of candied webbing as white and misty as the veil of the bride. It was the opening cotillion party of the summer. The men came in blue cloth coats with brass buttons, buff waistcoats, and laced and ruffled shirts; the ladies came in white satins with ethereal silk overdresses, embroidered in the figure of a gold beetle or an oak leaf of green. The walls of the ballroom were painted to represent landscapes of blooming orange trees, set here and there in clustering tubs; and the chandeliers and sconces were lighted with innumerable wax candles, yellow and green and rose.

Only the day before, also, Clatterbuck had opened for the summer a new villa-house, six miles out in the country, with a dancing pavilion in a grove of maples and oaks, a pleasure boat on a sheet of crystal water, and a cellar stocked with old sherry, Sauterne, and Chateau Margaux wines, with anisette, "Perfect Love," and Guigholet cordials.

Down on Water Street, near where now stands a railway station, Hugh Lonney, urging that the fear of cholera was not the only incentive to cleanliness, had just fitted up a sumptuous bathhouse, where cold and shower baths might be had at twelve and a half cents each, or hot ones at three for half a dollar.

Recalling Facts

1. Virginia and Tennessee were suffering from
   - ☐ a. ice storms.
   - ☐ b. drought.
   - ☐ c. locusts.

2. Lake Erie was
   - ☐ a. rising past the flood plains.
   - ☐ b. blocked with ice.
   - ☐ c. filled with debris.

3. M. Giron made
   - ☐ a. wedding gowns.
   - ☐ b. candies and cookies.
   - ☐ c. musical instruments.

4. The new villa-house was opened by
   - ☐ a. Clatterbuck.
   - ☐ b. M. Giron.
   - ☐ c. M. Xaupi.

5. Hugh Lonney opened up a new
   - ☐ a. wine cellar.
   - ☐ b. boat dock.
   - ☐ c. bathhouse.

Understanding the Passage

6. The weather during the year had been
   - ☐ a. warmer than usual.
   - ☐ b. unusually calm.
   - ☐ c. bizarre.

7. The apple crop in Kentucky was wiped out by a
   - ☐ a. spring frost.
   - ☐ b. swarm of caterpillars.
   - ☐ c. strange virus.

8. The great ball probably took place in
   - ☐ a. October.
   - ☐ b. June.
   - ☐ c. January.

9. The cotillion party was
   - ☐ a. formal.
   - ☐ b. semiformal.
   - ☐ c. casual.

10. Cholera was
   - ☐ a. a thing of the past.
   - ☐ b. a serious concern.
   - ☐ c. unknown in this region.

It was past the middle of the fifteen century, Louis XI was sovereign of France; Edward IV was wrongful King of England; and Philip "the Good," having by force and cunning dispossessed his cousin Jacqueline, and broken her heart, reigned undisturbed this many years in Holland, where our tale begins.

Elias, and Catherine his wife, lived in the little town of Tergou. He traded, wholesale and retail, in cloth, silk, brown holland, and above all, in curried leather, a material highly valued by the middling people, because it would stand twenty years' wear, and turn an ordinary knife, no small virtue in a jerkin of that century, in which folk were so liberal of their steel; even at dinner a man would leave his meat awhile, and carve you his neighbor, on a very moderate difference of opinion.

The couple were well-to-do, and would have been free from all earthly care, but for nine children. When these were coming into the world, one per annum, each was hailed with rejoicings, and the saints were thanked, not expostulated with; and when parents and children were all young together, the latter were looked upon as lovely little playthings invented by Heaven for the amusement, joy, and evening solace of people in business.

But as the olive branches shot up, and the parents grew older, and saw with their own eyes the fate of large families, misgivings and care mingled with their love. They belonged to a singularly wise and provident people: in Holland reckless parents were as rare as disobedient children. So now when the huge loaf came in on a gigantic trencher, looking like a fortress in its moat, and, the tour of the table made once, it seemed to have melted away, Elias and Catherine would look at one another and say, "Who is to find bread for them all when we are gone?"

At this observation the younger ones needed all their filial respect to keep their little Dutch countenances; for in their opinion dinner and supper came by nature like sunrise and sunset, and, so long as that luminary should travel round the earth, so long *must* the brown loaf go round their family circle, and set in their stomachs only to rise again in the family oven. But the remark awakened the national thoughtfulness of the elder boys, and being often repeated, set several of the family thinking.

Recalling Facts

1. This story is set in
   - ☐ a. France.
   - ☐ b. England.
   - ☐ c. Holland.

2. Elias and Catherine lived between
   - ☐ a. 1400–1500.
   - ☐ b. 1500–1600.
   - ☐ c. 1700–1800.

3. Elias worked as a
   - ☐ a. tanner.
   - ☐ b. merchant.
   - ☐ c. weaver.

4. Elias and Catherine had
   - ☐ a. three children.
   - ☐ b. five children.
   - ☐ c. nine children.

5. The symbol for food in this family was
   - ☐ a. brown bread.
   - ☐ b. deer and game birds.
   - ☐ c. rice pudding.

Understanding the Passage

6. The narrator did not have a high opinion of
   - ☐ a. any monarch.
   - ☐ b. Louis XI.
   - ☐ c. Edward IV.

7. Curried leather was highly valued because
   - ☐ a. it wore so well.
   - ☐ b. it was hard to penetrate with a knife.
   - ☐ c. both a and b.

8. Life at this time was apparently
   - ☐ a. peaceful and prosperous.
   - ☐ b. rather violent.
   - ☐ c. based on democratic values.

9. Children in Tergou were
   - ☐ a. generally well behaved.
   - ☐ b. hard to please at dinnertime.
   - ☐ c. both a and b.

10. The younger children believed that
    - ☐ a. their parents would soon be gone.
    - ☐ b. the family would never run out of food.
    - ☐ c. the older children were too serious.

Don Ippolito had slept upon his interview with Ferris, and now sat in his laboratory, amidst the many witnesses of his inventive industry, with the model of the breech loading cannon on the workbench before him. He had neatly mounted it on wheels that its completeness might do him the greater credit with the consul when he should show it him, but the carriage had been broken in his pocket, on the way home, by an unlucky thrust from the burden of a porter, and the poor toy lay there disabled, as if to dramatize that premature explosion in the secret chamber.

His heart was in these inventions of his, which had as yet so grudgingly repaid his affection. For their sake he had stinted himself of many needful things. The meager stipend which he received from the patrimony of his church, eked out with the money paid him for baptisms, funerals and marriages, and for masses by people who had friends to be prayed out of purgatory, would at best have barely sufficed to support him; but he denied himself everything save the necessary decorums of dress and lodging; he fasted like a saint, and slept hard as a hermit that he might spend upon these ungrateful creatures of his brain. They were the work of his own hands, and so he saved the expense of their construction, but there were many little outlays for materials and for tools, which he could not avoid, and with him a little was all. They not only famished him; they isolated him. His superiors in the church and his brother priests looked with doubt or ridicule upon the labors for which he shunned their company, while he gave up the other social joys, few and small, which a priest might know in the Venice of that day, when all generous spirits regarded him with suspicion for his cloth's sake, and church and state were alert to detect disaffection or indifference in him. But bearing these things willingly, and living as frugally as he might, he had still not enough, and he had been fain to assume the instruction of a young girl of old and noble family in certain branches of polite learning which a young lady of that sort might fitly know. The family was not so rich as it was old and noble, and Don Ippolito was paid from its purse rather than its pride.

Recalling Facts

1. Don Ippolito had a toy model of a
   - ☐ a. gondola.
   - ☐ b. tiny church.
   - ☐ c. breech loading cannon.

2. Don Ippolito's toy model was accidentally broken by
   - ☐ a. a porter.
   - ☐ b. a friend.
   - ☐ c. Ferris.

3. Don Ippolito made some money by
   - ☐ a. presiding at funerals and marriages.
   - ☐ b. working part-time in the kitchen.
   - ☐ c. working in the church gardens.

4. Colleagues viewed Don Ippolito's work with
   - ☐ a. doubt.
   - ☐ b. envy.
   - ☐ c. reverence.

5. Don Ippolito tutored a young girl from a
   - ☐ a. poor but noble family.
   - ☐ b. poor peasant family.
   - ☐ c. wealthy, noble family.

Understanding the Passage

6. Don Ippolito's many inventions
   - ☐ a. earned him widespread acclaim.
   - ☐ b. had not earned him much money.
   - ☐ c. were destroyed in an explosion.

7. Don Ippolito's greatest love appeared to be
   - ☐ a. conducting church services.
   - ☐ b. teaching.
   - ☐ c. inventing.

8. Don Ippolito's lifestyle can best be described as
   - ☐ a. bleak and spartan.
   - ☐ b. full of adventure.
   - ☐ c. soft and luxurious.

9. Church officials thought Don Ippolito
   - ☐ a. was a fine priest.
   - ☐ b. might not have his heart in his work.
   - ☐ c. socialized too much with other priests.

10. Don Ippolito began tutoring the young girl because
    - ☐ a. he enjoyed teaching.
    - ☐ b. the family specifically asked for him.
    - ☐ c. he needed more money to live on.

45 *from* The Adventures of Harry Richmond *by George Meredith*

From that hour till the day Heriot's aunt came to see me, I lived systematically out of myself in extreme flights of imagination, locking my doors up, as it were, all the faster for the extremest strokes of Mr. Rippenger's rod. He remarked justly that I grew an impenetrably sullen boy, a constitutional rebel, a callous lump, and assured me that if my father would not pay for me, I at least should not escape my debts. The title of "little impostor," transmitted from the master's mouth to the school in designation of one who had come to him as a young prince, and for whom he had not received one penny's indemnification, naturally caused me to have fights with several of the boys. Whereupon I was reported: I was prayed at to move my spirit, and flogged to exercise my flesh. The floggings, after they were over, crowned me with delicious sensations of martyrdom—even while the sting lasted I could say, it's for Heriot and Julia! And it gave me a wonderful penetration into the mournful ecstasy of love. Julia was sent away to a relative by the seaside, because, one of the housemaids told me, she could not bear to hear of my being beaten. Mr. Rippenger summoned me to his private room to bid me inform him whether I had other relatives besides my father, such as grandfather, grandmother, uncles, or aunt, or a mother. I daresay Julia would have led me to break my word to my father by speaking of old Riversley, a place I half longed for since my father had grown so distant and dim to me, but confession to Mr. Rippenger seemed, as he said of Heriot's behavior to him, a gross breach of trust to my father; so I refused steadily to answer, and suffered the consequences now on my dear father's behalf.

Heriot's aunt brought me a cake, and in a letter from him an extraordinary sum of money for a boy of my age. The money was like a golden gate through which freedom twinkled a finger. Forthwith I paid my debts, amounting to two pounds twelve shillings, and instructed a couple of day boarders, commercial fellows, whose heavy and mysterious charges for commissions ran up a bill in no time, to prepare to bring us materials for a feast on Saturday.

Recalling Facts

1. Mr. Rippenger claimed that the narrator had become
   - ☐ a. sullen.
   - ☐ b. cooperative.
   - ☐ c. indifferent.

2. The narrator's father had
   - ☐ a. never seen his son.
   - ☐ b. never paid his son's tuition.
   - ☐ c. both a and b.

3. The narrator's usual punishment was
   - ☐ a. detention.
   - ☐ b. flogging.
   - ☐ c. extra work.

4. The narrator refused to answer most questions about his
   - ☐ a. fighting.
   - ☐ b. studies.
   - ☐ c. family.

5. Heriot sent the narrator
   - ☐ a. money.
   - ☐ b. a cake.
   - ☐ c. a feast.

Understanding the Passage

6. Mr. Rippenger did not like
   - ☐ a. running a school.
   - ☐ b. flogging boys.
   - ☐ c. the narrator's attitude.

7. Julia became distressed whenever
   - ☐ a. Heriot gave money away.
   - ☐ b. she heard of the narrator's beatings.
   - ☐ c. cake was served to the boys.

8. The nickname of the "little impostor"
   - ☐ a. pleased the narrator.
   - ☐ b. upset the narrator.
   - ☐ c. upset Julia.

9. Until Heriot's aunt came to see him, the narrator had
   - ☐ a. good grades.
   - ☐ b. no money.
   - ☐ c. severe headaches.

10. The narrator did not want to
    - ☐ a. attend the Saturday feast.
    - ☐ b. keep secrets from Mr. Rippenger.
    - ☐ c. betray his father.

Harry Warrington and his brother pored over the English map and determined upon the course which they should take upon arriving at Home. All Americans who love the old country—and what gently nurtured man or woman of Anglo-Saxon race does not?—have ere this rehearsed their English travels, and visited in fancy the spots with which their hopes, their parents' fond stories, their friends' descriptions, have rendered them familiar. There are few things to me more affecting in the history of the quarrel which divided the two great nations than that word Home, as used by the younger towards the elder country. Harry Warrington had his chart laid out. Before London, and its glorious temples of St. Paul's and St. Peter's, and its grim Tower, where the brave and loyal had shed their blood, from Wallace down to Balmerino and Kilmarnock, pitied by gentle hearts;—before the awful window at Whitehall, whence the martyr Charles had issued, to kneel once more, and then ascend to heaven;—before Playhouses, Parks, and Palaces, wondrous resorts of wit, pleasure, and splendor;—before Shakespeare's resting place under the tall spire which rises by Avon, amidst the sweet Warwickshire pastures;—before Derby, and Falkirk, and Culloden, where the cause of honor and loyalty had fallen, it might be to rise no more—before all these points in their pilgrimage there was one which the young Virginian brothers held even more sacred, and that was the home of their family—that old Castlewood in Hampshire, about which their parents had talked so fondly. From Bristol to Bath, from Bath to Salisbury, to Winchester, to Kexton, to *Home*—they knew the way and had mapped the journey many and many a time.

We must fancy our American traveler to be a handsome young fellow whose suit of sables only made him look the more interesting. The plump landlady from her bar, surrounded by her china and punch bowls, and stout gilded bottles of strong waters, and glittering rows of silver flagons, looked kindly after the young gentleman as he passed through the inn hall and the obsequious chamberlain bowed him up stairs to the "Rose" or the "Dolphin." The trim chambermaid dropped her best curtsy for his fee, and Gumbo, in the inn kitchen, where the townsfolk drank their mug of ale by the great fire, bragged of his young master's splendid house in Virginia and of the immense wealth to which he was heir.

Recalling Facts

1. Harry Warrington and his brother were about to visit
   □ a. Virginia.
   □ b. New Hampshire.
   □ c. England.

2. The narrator was most affected by the word
   □ a. Tower.
   □ b. Home.
   □ c. Shakespeare.

3. The cause of honor and loyalty had fallen at
   □ a. Culloden.
   □ b. Bristol.
   □ c. Balmerino.

4. The place held most sacred by the brothers was
   □ a. old Castlewood.
   □ b. Bath.
   □ c. Kexton.

5. Harry had a splendid home in
   □ a. London.
   □ b. Winchester.
   □ c. Virginia.

Understanding the Passage

6. Harry was
   □ a. delaying his trip.
   □ b. trying to postpone his trip.
   □ c. eagerly awaiting his trip.

7. Many people died at
   □ a. the Tower.
   □ b. St. Paul's.
   □ c. Wallace.

8. Apparently, Charles
   □ a. died heroically.
   □ b. was extremely witty.
   □ c. traveled to Virginia.

9. The parents of the two brothers were
   □ a. quite poor.
   □ b. raised in England.
   □ c. born in New England.

10. The servants appeared to be
    □ a. envious of Harry's wealth.
    □ b. impressed with Harry's wealth.
    □ c. too busy drinking to notice Harry.

The history of Iván Ilyitch's past life was most simple and uneventful, and yet most terrible.

Iván Ilyitch died at the age of forty-five, a member of the Court of Justice. He was the son of a government official, who had followed, in various ministries at Petersburg, a career such as brings men into a position from which, on account of their long service and their rank, they are never turned adrift, even though it is plainly manifest that their actual usefulness is at an end; and consequently they obtain imaginary, fictitious places, and from six to ten thousand that are not fictitious, on which they live till a good old age.

Such was Ilyá Yefimovitch Golovin, privy councillor, the useless member of various useless commissions.

He had three sons: Iván Ilyitch was the second son. The eldest had followed the same career as his father's, but in a different ministry, and was already nearing that period of his service in which inertia carries a man into emoluments. The third son had made a flash in the pan. He had failed completely in several positions, and he was now connected with railroads; and his father and brothers not only disliked to meet him, but, except when it was absolutely necessary, even forgot that he existed.

A sister was married to Baron Gref, who, like his father-in-law, was a Petersburg government official. Iván Ilyitch was neither as chilly and accurate as the eldest brother, nor as unpromising as the youngest. He held the golden mean between them—an intelligent, lively, agreeable, and polished man. He had studied at the law school with his younger brother. The younger did not graduate, but was expelled from the fifth class; but Iván Ilyitch finished his course creditably. At the law school, he showed the same characteristics by which he was afterwards distinguished all his life: he was capable, good natured even to gaiety, and sociable, but strictly fulfilling all that he considered to be his duty: duty, in his opinion, was all that is considered to be such by men in the highest station. He was not one to curry favor, either as a boy, or afterwards in manhood, but from his earliest years he had been attracted by men in the highest station in society, just as a fly is by the light. He adopted their ways, their views of life, and entered into relations of friendship with them.

Recalling Facts

1. When Iván Ilyitch died he was a
   - ☐ a. government official.
   - ☐ b. member of the Court of Justice.
   - ☐ c. prime minister.

2. Iván's father was
   - ☐ a. a privy councillor.
   - ☐ b. the mayor of Petersburg.
   - ☐ c. a law school instructor.

3. Ilyá most disliked his
   - ☐ a. oldest son.
   - ☐ b. middle son.
   - ☐ c. youngest son.

4. Baron Gref held the same kind of position as his
   - ☐ a. sister.
   - ☐ b. father-in-law.
   - ☐ c. uncle.

5. Iván studied at
   - ☐ a. business school.
   - ☐ b. medical school.
   - ☐ c. law school.

Understanding the Passage

6. At the end of his career, Ilyá was
   - ☐ a. an important minister in St. Petersburg.
   - ☐ b. paid well for doing little.
   - ☐ c. kicked out of the ministry.

7. Ilyá's oldest son
   - ☐ a. followed in Ilyá's footsteps.
   - ☐ b. went to law school.
   - ☐ c. was about to become a major politician.

8. Iván could best be described as
   - ☐ a. temperate and well mannered.
   - ☐ b. a failure at most things.
   - ☐ c. calculating and ambitious.

9. As a student, Iván was
   - ☐ a. at the top of his class.
   - ☐ b. average.
   - ☐ c. at the bottom of his class.

10. Iván tended to seek out the company of those
    - ☐ a. below his social class.
    - ☐ b. from his own social class.
    - ☐ c. above his social class.

In that part of the western division of this kingdom which is commonly called Somersetshire, there lately lived and perhaps lives still, a gentleman whose name was Allworthy, and who might well be called the favorite of both Nature and Fortune, for both of these seem to have contended which should bless and enrich him most. In this contention Nature may seem to some to have come off victorious, as she bestowed on him many gifts, while Fortune had only one gift in her power; but in pouring forth this, she was so very profuse, that others perhaps may think this single endowment to have been more than equivalent to all the various blessings which he enjoyed from Nature. From the former of these he derived an agreeable person, a sound constitution, a sane understanding, and a benevolent heart; by the latter, he was decreed to the inheritance of one of the largest estates in the county.

This gentleman had in his youth married a very worthy and beautiful woman, of whom he had been extremely fond; by her he had three children, all of whom died in their infancy. He had likewise had the misfortune of burying this beloved wife herself, about five years before the time in which this history chooses to set out. This loss, however great, he bore like a man of sense and constancy, though it must be confessed he would often talk a little whimsically on this head; for he sometimes said he looked on himself as still married, and considered his wife as only gone a little before him, a journey which he should most certainly, sooner or later, take after her; and that he had not the least doubt of meeting her again in a place where he should never part with her more—sentiments for which his sense was arraigned by one part of his neighbors, his religion by a second, and his sincerity by a third.

He now lived, for the most part, retired in the country, with one sister, for whom he had a very tender affection. This lady was now somewhat past the age of thirty, an era at which, in the opinon of the malicious, the title of old maid may with no impropriety be assumed. She was of that species of women whom you commend rather for good qualities than beauty.

Recalling Facts

1. Somersetshire was located in the
   - ☐ a. south.
   - ☐ b. west.
   - ☐ c. east.

2. Allworthy was
   - ☐ a. cursed by Nature.
   - ☐ b. blessed by Nature alone.
   - ☐ c. blessed by Nature and Fortune.

3. Allworthy had a
   - ☐ a. good heart.
   - ☐ b. weak body.
   - ☐ c. morbid personality.

4. Allworthy's three children
   - ☐ a. died very young.
   - ☐ b. had constant colds.
   - ☐ c. were all boys.

5. Allworthy's sister
   - ☐ a. lived with Allworthy.
   - ☐ b. was regarded by many as an old maid.
   - ☐ c. both a and b.

Understanding the Passage

6. In terms of Nature and Fortune, Allworthy appeared to have been
   - ☐ a. unfortunate.
   - ☐ b. lucky.
   - ☐ c. cheated.

7. Allworthy's personal life was marred by
   - ☐ a. family tragedies.
   - ☐ b. financial setbacks.
   - ☐ c. unfriendly neighbors.

8. Allworthy apparently believed in
   - ☐ a. religious cultism.
   - ☐ b. an afterlife.
   - ☐ c. external damnation.

9. Allworthy's sister had
   - ☐ a. great beauty.
   - ☐ b. a nice personality.
   - ☐ c. no money of her own.

10. After his wife died, Allworthy
    - ☐ a. never spoke of her again.
    - ☐ b. eventually remarried.
    - ☐ c. continued to think of her.

It was after the early suppertime at the Red House, and the entertainment was in that stage when bashfulness itself had passed into easy jollity, when gentlemen, conscious of unusual accomplishments, could at length be prevailed on to dance a hornpipe, and when the Squire preferred talking loudly, scattering snuff, and patting his visitors' backs, to sitting longer at the whist table—a choice exasperating to Uncle Kimble, who, being always volatile in sober business hours, became intense and bitter over cards and brandy, shuffled before his adversary's deal with a glare of suspicion, and turned up a mean trump card with an air of inexpressible disgust, as if in a world where such things could happen one might as well enter on a course of reckless profligacy. When the evening had advanced to this pitch of freedom and enjoyment, it was usual for the servants to get their share of amusement by coming to look on at the dancing; so that the back regions of the house were left in solitude.

There were two doors by which the White Parlor was entered from the hall; but the lower one was crowded with the servants and villagers, and only the upper doorway was left free. Bob Cass was figuring in a hornpipe, and his father, very proud of this lithe son, whom he repeatedly declared to be just like himself in his young days in a tone that implied this to be the very highest stamp of juvenile merit, was the center of a group who had placed themselves opposite the performer, not far from the upper door. Godfrey was standing a little way off to keep sight of Nancy, who was seated in the group, near her father. He stood aloof, because he wished to avoid suggesting himself as a subject for the Squire's fatherly jokes in connection with matrimony and Miss Nancy Lammeter's beauty, which were likely to become more and more explicit. But he had the prospect of dancing with her again when the hornpipe was concluded, and in the meanwhile it was very pleasant to get long glances at her quite unobserved.

But when Godfrey was lifting his eyes from one of those long glances, they encountered an object as startling to him at that moment as if it had been an apparition from the dead. It was his own child carried in Silas Marner's arms.

Recalling Facts

1. After the early suppertime, the Squire preferred to
   - ☐ a. talk loudly.
   - ☐ b. sit still.
   - ☐ c. play cards.

2. During card games, Uncle Kimble became
   - ☐ a. a friendly back-slapper.
   - ☐ b. intense and bitter.
   - ☐ c. quiet and moody.

3. After a while, the servants
   - ☐ a. went home.
   - ☐ b. came to watch the dancing.
   - ☐ c. joined the dancers.

4. Nancy sat
   - ☐ a. by the lower door.
   - ☐ b. next to Godfrey.
   - ☐ c. near her father.

5. Godfrey saw his own child
   - ☐ a. in Silas's arms.
   - ☐ b. playing a hornpipe.
   - ☐ c. sleeping by a crowded doorway.

Understanding the Passage

6. The entertainment had apparently
   - ☐ a. just begun.
   - ☐ b. been going on for some time.
   - ☐ c. been centered around the whist game.

7. When playing cards, Uncle Kimble
   - ☐ a. was explosive and violent.
   - ☐ b. did not act as he usually did.
   - ☐ c. urged other players to cheat.

8. The servants got their entertainment by
   - ☐ a. watching the rich people at play.
   - ☐ b. dancing in the back rooms.
   - ☐ c. drinking with the Squire.

9. Mr. Cass thought very highly of
   - ☐ a. his son's ability.
   - ☐ b. his daughter's ability.
   - ☐ c. both a and b.

10. The Squire can best be described as
    - ☐ a. shy but pleasant.
    - ☐ b. sober but violently explosive.
    - ☐ c. humorous and fun loving.

For the young men of Cologne, Gottlieb had a high claim to reverence as father of the fair Margarita, the White Rose of Germany: a noble maiden, peerless, and a jewel for princes.

The devotion of these youths should give them a name in chivalry. In her honor, daily and nightly, they earned among themselves black bruises and paraded discolored faces, with the humble hope to find it pleasing in her sight. The tender fanatics went in bands up and down Rhineland, challenging wayfarers and the peasantry with staff and beaker to acknowledge the supremacy of their mistress. Whenever one of them journeyed into foreign parts, he wrote home boasting how many times his head had been broken on behalf of the fair Margarita; and if this happened very often, a spirit of envy was created, which compelled him, when he returned, to verify his prowess on no less than a score of his rivals. Not to possess a beauty scar, as the wounds received in these endless combats were called, became the sign of inferiority; so that much voluntary maiming was conjectured to be going on, and to obviate this piece of treachery, minutes of fights were taken and attested, setting forth that a certain glorious cut or crack was honorably won in fair field, on what occasion, and from whom; every member of the White Rose Club keeping his particular scroll, and, on days of festival and holiday, wearing it haughtily in his helm. Strangers entering Cologne were shocked at the hideous appearance of the striplings, and thought they never had observed so ugly a race, but they were forced to admit the fine influence of beauty on commerce, seeing that the consumption of beer increased almost hourly. All Bavaria could not equal Cologne for quantity made away with.

The chief members of the White Rose Club were Berthold Schmidt, the rich goldsmith's son; Dietrich Schill, son of the imperial saddler; Heinrich Abt, Franz Endermann, and Ernst Geller, sons of chief burghers, each of whom carried a yard-long scroll in his cap, and was too disfigured in person for men to require an inspection of the document. They were dangerous youths to meet, for the oaths, ceremonies, and recantations they demanded from every wayfarer, under the rank of baron, were what few might satisfactorily perform, and what none save trained heads and stomachs could withstand, however naturally manful.

Recalling Facts

1. Gottlieb was the fair
   Margarita's
   □ a. only detractor.
   □ b. father.
   □ c. lover.

2. On behalf of Margarita, the
   young men of Cologne
   □ a. got into many fights.
   □ b. wrote epic poems.
   □ c. sang love ballads.

3. It was a sign of inferiority to
   □ a. consume beer.
   □ b. travel overseas.
   □ c. have no beauty scar.

4. To strangers, the young men
   of Cologne appeared
   □ a. handsome.
   □ b. small and weak.
   □ c. ugly.

5. The young men confronted
   every wayfarer under the
   rank of
   □ a. general.
   □ b. knight.
   □ c. baron.

Understanding the Passage

6. The fair Margarita was
   □ a. married.
   □ b. widowed.
   □ c. single.

7. The young men of the White
   Rose Club wanted to impress
   □ a. strangers.
   □ b. Margarita.
   □ c. the king.

8. It was suspected that some
   members of the White
   Rose Club
   □ a. deliberately injured
        themselves.
   □ b. were actually cowards.
   □ c. really hated Margarita.

9. The members of the White
   Rose Club
   □ a. rarely drank beer.
   □ b. kept a record of
        each fight.
   □ c. spent most of their time
        in Bavaria.

10. The chief members of the
    White Rose Club came from
    □ a. wealthy Cologne families.
    □ b. Bavarian peasant families.
    □ c. families without fathers.

Answer Key

Progress Graph

Pacing Graph

Answer Key

1	1. a	2. b	3. b	4. a	5. a	6. a	7. b	8. c	9. b	10. a
2	1. c	2. a	3. c	4. a	5. c	6. b	7. a	8. a	9. c	10. b
3	1. b	2. c	3. b	4. a	5. b	6. a	7. a	8. a	9. b	10. a
4	1. b	2. b	3. b	4. a	5. c	6. a	7. c	8. b	9. b	10. a
5	1. c	2. c	3. b	4. b	5. a	6. a	7. c	8. a	9. c	10. c
6	1. c	2. b	3. b	4. b	5. c	6. b	7. a	8. a	9. a	10. b
7	1. a	2. b	3. b	4. b	5. a	6. c	7. a	8. a	9. c	10. c
8	1. c	2. b	3. a	4. b	5. c	6. b	7. c	8. a	9. a	10. c
9	1. a	2. c	3. c	4. a	5. a	6. c	7. c	8. a	9. b	10. a
10	1. b	2. c	3. a	4. a	5. c	6. a	7. b	8. b	9. c	10. c
11	1. c	2. b	3. a	4. a	5. b	6. b	7. a	8. b	9. a	10. b
12	1. b	2. c	3. a	4. a	5. c	6. b	7. b	8. c	9. c	10. c
13	1. c	2. a	3. c	4. b	5. c	6. b	7. a	8. c	9. b	10. a
14	1. b	2. c	3. c	4. a	5. a	6. c	7. c	8. c	9. b	10. b
15	1. b	2. c	3. b	4. c	5. c	6. a	7. a	8. c	9. b	10. a
16	1. b	2. a	3. a	4. b	5. c	6. a	7. c	8. b	9. b	10. b
17	1. b	2. c	3. c	4. a	5. a	6. b	7. a	8. b	9. a	10. a
18	1. b	2. b	3. b	4. b	5. a	6. a	7. b	8. a	9. a	10. c
19	1. c	2. c	3. a	4. b	5. c	6. b	7. a	8. c	9. a	10. c
20	1. b	2. a	3. b	4. b	5. b	6. a	7. a	8. b	9. b	10. c
21	1. b	2. c	3. c	4. a	5. a	6. b	7. c	8. a	9. a	10. c
22	1. c	2. c	3. c	4. a	5. b	6. c	7. b	8. b	9. c	10. a
23	1. a	2. c	3. c	4. c	5. c	6. a	7. a	8. b	9. b	10. a
24	1. a	2. b	3. b	4. b	5. c	6. b	7. b	8. c	9. a	10. a
25	1. c	2. b	3. a	4. c	5. c	6. a	7. b	8. c	9. a	10. a

26	1. c	2. a	3. c	4. b	5. a	6. c	7. b	8. b	9. b	10. a
27	1. b	2. a	3. c	4. c	5. a	6. a	7. b	8. c	9. b	10. c
28	1. b	2. c	3. a	4. c	5. c	6. a	7. b	8. a	9. a	10. b
29	1. c	2. b	3. b	4. b	5. b	6. a	7. c	8. a	9. a	10. b
30	1. a	2. c	3. a	4. c	5. b	6. b	7. b	8. a	9. a	10. b
31	1. b	2. c	3. a	4. a	5. c	6. c	7. c	8. b	9. a	10. b
32	1. a	2. c	3. c	4. a	5. c	6. b	7. a	8. a	9. a	10. c
33	1. a	2. c	3. a	4. b	5. c	6. b	7. a	8. b	9. a	10. a
34	1. b	2. a	3. c	4. b	5. c	6. b	7. a	8. a	9. c	10. b
35	1. a	2. b	3. c	4. a	5. b	6. b	7. b	8. b	9. a	10. a
36	1. b	2. c	3. a	4. a	5. c	6. b	7. a	8. a	9. a	10. c
37	1. a	2. b	3. c	4. a	5. c	6. a	7. a	8. b	9. c	10. c
38	1. b	2. c	3. c	4. a	5. a	6. b	7. a	8. a	9. c	10. b
39	1. b	2. c	3. a	4. a	5. c	6. b	7. a	8. c	9. c	10. c
40	1. b	2. c	3. a	4. c	5. b	6. a	7. b	8. a	9. c	10. c
41	1. c	2. a	3. a	4. a	5. b	6. a	7. a	8. b	9. a	10. a
42	1. c	2. b	3. b	4. a	5. c	6. c	7. b	8. b	9. a	10. b
43	1. c	2. a	3. b	4. c	5. a	6. c	7. c	8. b	9. a	10. b
44	1. c	2. a	3. a	4. a	5. a	6. b	7. c	8. a	9. b	10. c
45	1. a	2. b	3. b	4. c	5. a	6. c	7. b	8. b	9. b	10. c
46	1. c	2. b	3. a	4. a	5. c	6. c	7. a	8. a	9. b	10. b
47	1. b	2. a	3. c	4. b	5. c	6. b	7. a	8. a	9. b	10. c
48	1. b	2. c	3. a	4. a	5. c	6. b	7. a	8. b	9. b	10. c
49	1. a	2. b	3. b	4. c	5. a	6. b	7. b	8. a	9. a	10. c
50	1. b	2. a	3. c	4. c	5. c	6. c	7. b	8. a	9. b	10. a

Progress Graph (1–25)

Directions: Write your comprehension score in the box under the selection number. Then put an x on the line above each box to show your reading time and words-per-minute reading rate.

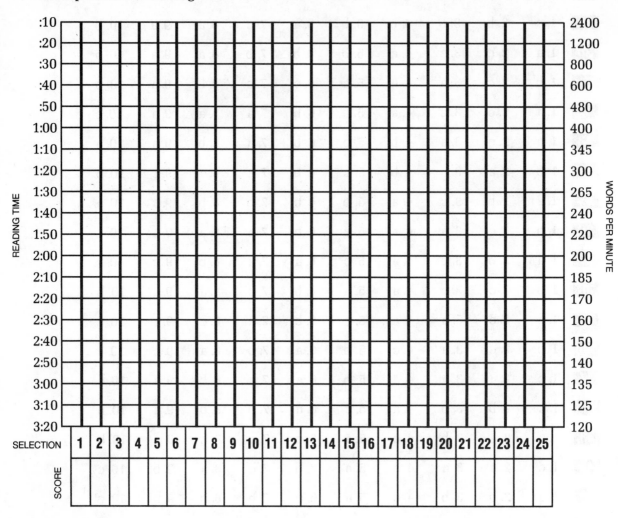

READING TIME		WORDS PER MINUTE
:10		2400
:20		1200
:30		800
:40		600
:50		480
1:00		400
1:10		345
1:20		300
1:30		265
1:40		240
1:50		220
2:00		200
2:10		185
2:20		170
2:30		160
2:40		150
2:50		140
3:00		135
3:10		125
3:20		120

SELECTION: 1 2 3 4 5 6 7 8 9 10 11 12 13 14 15 16 17 18 19 20 21 22 23 24 25

SCORE

Progress Graph (26–50)

Directions: Write your comprehension score in the box under the selection number. Then put an x on the line above each box to show your reading time and words-per-minute reading rate.

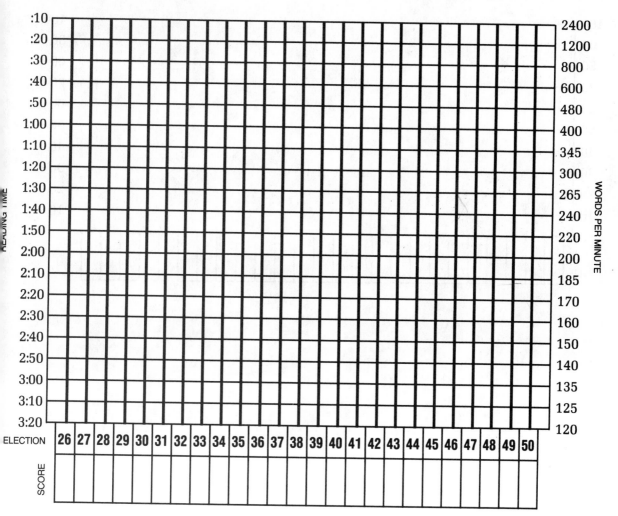

Pacing Graph

Directions: In the boxes labeled "Pace" along the bottom of the graph, write your words-per-minute rate. On the vertical line above each box, put an x to indicate your comprehension score.

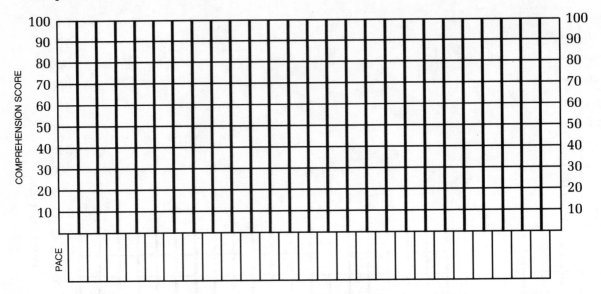